Mammy сночку, чтобы
он полюбил science.
We will have FUN
doing all these
projects this summer.
I love you soooo
much, Nick. Be a
smart, kind and happy!

love,

mom

2011

A+ ACE YOUR BIOLOGY SCIENCE PROJECT

ACE YOUR PLANT SCIENCE PROJECT

Robert Gardner
and
Phyllis J. Perry

GREAT SCIENCE FAIR IDEAS

Enslow Publishers, Inc.
40 Industrial Road
Box 398
Berkeley Heights, NJ 07922
USA

http://www.enslow.com

Library of Congress Cataloging-in-Publication Data

Gardner, Robert, 1929–
    Ace your plant science project : great science fair ideas / Robert Gardner and Phyllis J. Perry.
        p. cm. — (Ace your biology science project)
    Includes bibliographical references and index.
    Summary: "Presents several science experiments and project ideas using plants"—Provided by
        publisher.
    ISBN-13: 978-0-7660-3221-7
    ISBN-10: 0-7660-3221-3
    1. Botany—Experiments—Juvenile literature. 2. Plants—Experiments—Juvenile literature.
       3. Botany projects—Juvenile literature. I. Perry, Phyllis Jean. II. Title.
    QK52.6.G36 2009
    580.78—dc22

                                2008004687

Printed in the United States of America

10 9 8 7 6 5 4 3 2 1

To Our Readers: We have done our best to make sure all Internet Addresses in this book were active
and appropriate when we went to press. However, the author and the publisher have no control
over and assume no liability for the material available on those Internet sites or on other Web sites
they may link to. Any comments or suggestions can be sent by e-mail to comments@enslow.com or
to the address on the back cover.

♻ Enslow Publishers, Inc., is committed to printing our books on recycled paper. The paper in every
book contains 10% to 30% post-consumer waste (PCW). The cover board on the outside of each book
contains 100% PCW. Our goal is to do our part to help young people and the environment too!

The experiments in this book are a collection of the authors' best experiments, which were previously
published by Enslow Publishers, Inc. in *Science Fair Success With Plants*, *Science Project Ideas About
Trees*, and *Science Projects About Plants*.

Illustration Credits: © Duncan Astbury/iStockphoto.com, Figure 26; Stephen F. Delisle, Figures 2–16,
20; Jacob Katari, Figures 1, 17–19, 21–25, 27.

Photo Credits: © bubaone/iStockphoto.com, trophy icons; © Chen Fu Soh/iStockphoto.com, back-
grounds; © Izabela Habur/iStockphoto.com, p. 1 (girl); Shutterstock, pp. 1 (objects), 10, 28, 50, 95.

Cover Photos: © Izabela Habur/iStockphoto.com (girl); Shutterstock (objects).

CONTENTS

◐ *Indicates experiments that offer ideas for science fair projects.*

◔ *Indicates experiments that offer ideas for science fair projects.*

INTRODUCTION

When you hear the word *science*, do you think of a person in a white lab coat surrounded by beakers of bubbling liquids, specialized lab equipment, and computers? What exactly is science? Maybe you think science is only a subject you learn in school. Science is much more than that.

Science is the study of the things that are all around you, every day. No matter where you are or what you are doing, scientific principles are at work. You don't need special materials or equipment to be a scientist. Materials commonly found in your home, at school, or at a local store will allow you to become a scientist and pursue an area of interest. By making careful observations and asking questions about how things work, you can begin to design experiments to investigate a variety of questions. You can do science. You probably already have but just didn't know it!

Perhaps you are reading this book because you are looking for an idea for a science fair project for school, or maybe you are just hoping to find something fun to do on a rainy day. This book will provide an opportunity to conduct experiments and collect data to learn more about plants. Plants are different from all other living things because they make their own food in a process called *photosynthesis*. Plants are green because they contain a pigment called *chlorophyll*. Chlorophyll allows plants to absorb energy from sunlight. During photosynthesis, this light energy is used to produce sugar and oxygen from water and carbon dioxide. Excess sugar is stored as starch in plants. All other types of living things must eat plants or other animals in order to get their energy.

Plants have specialized structures called roots, stems, buds, and leaves. Each of these has a special job to do. Some plants have flowers; others have cones. Flowers and cones carry out reproduction and produce seeds. When a seed lands on favorable conditions, it germinates and becomes a seedling. The seedling pushes roots down into the ground. It produces a stem from which leaves bud. The seedling may grow into a small herb, a shrub, or a tree. Although plants have a lot in common, there are many different kinds of plants. The study of plants is called *botany*, and scientists who study plants are called botanists.

THE SCIENTIFIC METHOD

All scientists look at the world and try to understand how things work. They make careful observations and conduct research about a question. Different areas of science use different approaches. Depending on the phenomenon being investigated, one method is likely to be more appropriate than another. Designing a new medication for heart disease, studying the spread of an invasive plant species, such as purple loosestrife, and finding evidence about whether there was once water on Mars all require different methods.

Despite the differences, however, all scientists use a similar general approach to do experiments. It is called the scientific method. In most experiments, some or all of the following steps are used: making an observation, formulating a question, making a hypothesis (an answer to the question) and prediction (an if-then statement), designing and conducting an experiment, analyzing results and drawing conclusions, and accepting or rejecting the hypothesis. Scientists then share their findings with others by writing articles that are published in journals. After—and only after—a hypothesis has repeatedly been supported by experiments can it be considered a theory.

You might be wondering how to get an experiment started. When you observe something in the world, you may become curious and think of a question. Your question can be answered by a well-designed investigation. Your question may also arise from an earlier experiment or from background reading. Once you have a question, you should make a hypothesis. Your hypothesis is a possible answer to the question (what you think will happen). Once you have a hypothesis, it is time to design an experiment.

In many cases, it is appropriate to do a controlled experiment. That means there are two groups treated exactly the same except for the single factor that you are testing. Any factor that can affect the outcome of an experiment is a *variable*. In a controlled experiment, all variables are kept the same except for the one the experimenter wants to investigate. For example, if you want to investigate whether green plants need light to grow, two groups may be used. One group is called the control group, and the other is called the experimental group. The two groups of plants should be treated exactly the same: They should receive the same amount and type of soil and water, be kept at the same temperature, and so forth. The control group is the plants kept in the dark while the experimental group is the plants kept in the light. The variable of interest is light. It is the variable that changes, and it is the only difference between the two groups.

During the experiment, you will collect data. In this example, you might measure growth of the plants in centimeters or count the number of leaves. You might note color and condition of the leaves. By comparing the data collected from the control group with the data collected from the experimental group, you can draw conclusions. Because the two groups were treated exactly alike except for light, increased growth of plants kept in the light would allow you to conclude with confidence that more growth is a result of the one thing that was different: the availability of light.

Two other terms that are often used in scientific experiments are *dependent* and *independent* variables. The dependent variable here is growth, because it is the one you measure as an outcome. Light is the independent variable; it is the one the experimenter intentionally changes. After the data is collected, it is analyzed to see whether the hypothesis was supported or rejected. Often, the results of one experiment will lead you to a related question, or they may send you off in a different direction. Whatever the results, there is something to be learned from all scientific experiments.

SCIENCE FAIRS

Many of the experiments in this book may be appropriate for science fair projects. Experiments marked with a symbol (⬇) include a section called Science Fair Project Ideas. The ideas in this section provide suggestions to help you develop your own original science fair project. However, judges at such fairs do not reward projects or experiments that are simply copied from a book. For example, a model of a leaf or a flower, which is commonly found at these fairs, would probably not impress judges unless it was done in a novel way. On the other hand, a carefully performed experiment to find out how the removal of carbon dioxide from the air affects a plant growing under otherwise normal conditions would probably receive careful consideration.

Science fair judges tend to reward creative thought and imagination. However, it's difficult to be creative or imaginative unless you are really interested in your project. Take the time to choose a topic that really appeals to you. Consider, too, your own ability and the cost of materials. Don't pursue a project that you can't afford.

If you decide to use a project found in this book for a science fair, you will need to find ways to modify or extend it. That should not be difficult because you will probably find that as you do these projects new ideas for experiments will come to mind. These new experiments could make excellent science fair projects, particularly because they spring from your own mind and are interesting to you.

If you decide to enter a science fair and have never done so before, you should read some of the books listed in the "Further Reading" section. The books that deal specifically with science fairs will provide plenty of helpful hints and lots of useful information that will enable you to avoid the pitfalls that sometimes plague first-time entrants. You will learn how to prepare appealing reports that include charts and graphs, how to set up and display your work, how to present your project, and how to relate to judges and visitors.

SAFETY FIRST

As with many activities, safety is important in science and certain rules apply when conducting experiments. Some of the rules below may seem obvious to you, while others may not, but each is important to follow.

1. Have **an adult** help you whenever the book advises.

2. Wear eye protection and closed-toe shoes (rather than sandals) and tie back long hair.

3. Don't eat or drink while doing experiments and never taste substances being used.

4. Avoid touching chemicals.

5. Keep flammable substances away from fire.

6. Do only those experiments that are described in the book or those that have been approved by **a knowledgeable adult**.

7. Never engage in horseplay or play practical jokes.

8. Before beginning, read through the entire experimental procedure to make sure you understand all the instructions. Clear extra items from your work space.

9. At the end of every activity, clean all materials and put them away. Wash your hands thoroughly with soap and water.

Chapter 1

Seeds and Germination

SEEDS ARE PART OF THE LIFE CYCLE OF MANY GREEN PLANTS. A seed has a protective outer coating. Inside lies a tiny new plant, or *embryo*. Seeds also contain nutrients to provide energy for the developing embryo. A seed germinates to become a seedling (see Figure 1).

Under the right conditions seeds germinate and grow into mature plants that produce flowers or cones. The flowers or cones produce egg and sperm cells that join to form embryo plants. In plants such as pine trees, the naked seeds fall from their cones, but in other plants, particularly those we call vegetables or fruits, the seeds are surrounded by the ripened ovaries (fruit) of the flowers in which fertilization took place. When the fruit opens, is eaten, or decays, the seeds may fall on soil where they can germinate, and the cycle begins all over again.

Although many seeds germinate as soon as they receive water and are in warm temperatures, others sprout only after they pass through a resting stage known as dormancy. For many plants dormancy is an adaptation for survival. In climates that have cold winters, seedlings would soon die if they germinated during the autumn soon after they fell from the parent plants. By remaining dormant during months of cold weather, their chances of survival improve dramatically.

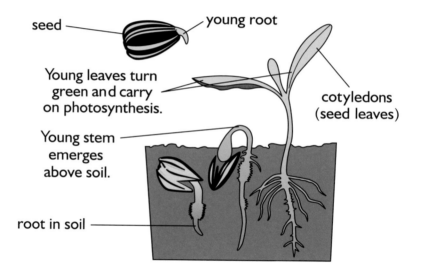

[FIGURE 1]

seed — young root

Young leaves turn green and carry on photosynthesis.

cotyledons (seed leaves)

Young stem emerges above soil.

root in soil

A seed germinates and becomes a seedling.

Often, seeds that pass through a dormant period have hard, thick coats through which water cannot pass. They have to be nicked in some way before water can enter the seed and induce germination. The nicking can be caused by natural forces, such as freezing and thawing, bacteria, or other factors. For seeds of significant agricultural importance, such as clover, machines with abrasive devices are used to scar their seed coats so that they will germinate when sown in moist soil.

The viability of seeds, or their ability to germinate, is lost after a period of time. Yet the period during which seeds are viable varies considerably. The seeds of some willows are viable for only a few days, while four-hundred-year-old Indian lotus seeds have germinated after being nicked and provided with moisture and warmth. Most seeds are viable for no more than ten years. Seeds stored under cool, dry conditions retain their viability longer than those stored in a warm, damp environment. Other seeds are dormant because certain slow chemical reactions must take place within them before they are ready to germinate.

In this chapter, you will watch seeds germinate and investigate factors that affect germination.

1.1 Watching Seeds Germinate

Materials:
- paper towels
- seeds (lima bean, corn, squash, pea, and others)
- large, clear drinking glass
- newspaper
- water

You can watch seeds in a glass germinate in much the same way that they would in soil. Line the walls of a large drinking glass with several paper towels as shown in Figure 2. Wet the towels so they will stick to the glass. Fill the rest of the glass with a crumpled sheet of newspaper. The newspaper will hold the towels in place. Pour water into the bottom of the glass until it is about 2 to 3 cm (1 in) deep. Capillary action will carry the water up the paper towel to keep it wet.

Now you are ready to "plant" the seeds. Place different kinds of seeds, several of each kind, between the moist towels and the glass. You might include corn, lima beans, peas, squash, and any others that are available. Orient the seeds in different ways—upside down, right side up, and sideways. You can prepare as many paper-towel-lined glasses as you wish.

How long does it take each kind of seed to germinate? Keep careful records. Which seeds germinate first? Which germinate last? Watch the seedlings after they have germinated. Do all the seedlings grow straight up? Can seeds that germinate in your "observatorium" be transplanted to soil and survive?

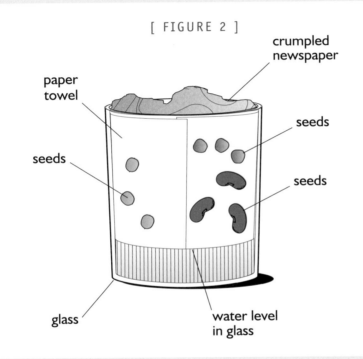

[FIGURE 2]

crumpled
newspaper

paper
towel

seeds

seeds

seeds

glass

water level
in glass

With a setup like this you can watch seeds germinate as they would in soil. Does their orientation affect their germination?

Materials:
- 4 wide, shallow trays
- paper towels
- water
- seeds (lima bean, navy bean, radish, corn, lentil, pea, and others)
- plastic wrap
- stick-on labels
- refrigerator
- warm room
- dark room or closet

Germinating seeds reveal the emergence of life from something that was previously dormant and seemingly lifeless. In this experiment you will determine what is needed to change an apparently inert seed into a growing seedling.

Cover the bottoms of four wide, shallow trays with two or three layers of paper towels. In three of the trays, dampen (don't soak) the towels with water. Place about a dozen seeds of each kind you want to germinate in separate regions on the towels in each tray. Then cover the trays with clear plastic wrap. Leave one end of the plastic loose so air can reach the seeds. The clear plastic covers will reduce the rate at which water evaporates from the towels while still allowing you to observe the seeds.

Apply stick-on labels to the plastic wrap so you can identify the seeds in the trays. Place one of the trays with damp towels in a refrigerator. Leave two trays—one with damp towels and one with dry towels—in a warm room. Place another tray with damp towels in a warm, dark room or closet. Check the seeds each day and add enough water to keep the damp towels moist. Add no water to the tray with the dry towel.

After watching the seeds for a few days, see if you can answer the following questions. Can seeds germinate without being placed in soil?

Is water essential for germination? Does temperature affect germination? If it does, how? Is light or darkness essential for seeds to germinate? Is either light or darkness essential for some kinds of seeds to germinate? Which seeds germinate quickly? Which seeds take a long time to germinate?

Science Fair Project Ideas

- Design an experiment to find out whether pea seeds will germinate in colder temperatures than corn seeds.
- Will the birdseed you buy in a store germinate? If the birdseed germinates, will it germinate in a refrigerator? Will it germinate in a freezer?

Materials:

- lima bean seeds
- water
- glass
- measuring teaspoon
- sugar
- 5 plastic cups
- salt
- honey
- paper towels
- 5 wide, plastic containers about 1-L (1 qt) capacity
- cardboard or plastic
- labels (Masking tape can be used.)
- starch
- clear plastic wrap

Cotyledons, or seed leaves, are the lowest leaves on a stem. Food stored in cotyledons allows the embryo inside the seed to grow. A plant's stem has its origin in the *epicotyl* of the seed's embryo (see Figure 3a). The plant's root develops from the embryo's *hypocotyl*. When a seed germinates, the end of the hypocotyl, which is called the *radicle*, is usually the first structure to emerge. This first root's entrance into soil, following the force of gravity, enables the germinating plant to absorb water and minerals before the seed's food supply is exhausted.

The emergence of the radicle is followed by the upward, gravity-defying movement of the epicotyl toward light and air. The stem provides the pathway by which water and minerals reach the leaves and other tissues. It also provides the support needed for leaves and flowers to develop.

A plant's primary root develops from the embryo's radicle and generally grows straight down into the soil. Shortly after the primary root begins its growth, it produces branches called secondary roots. The secondary roots grow horizontally as well as downward.

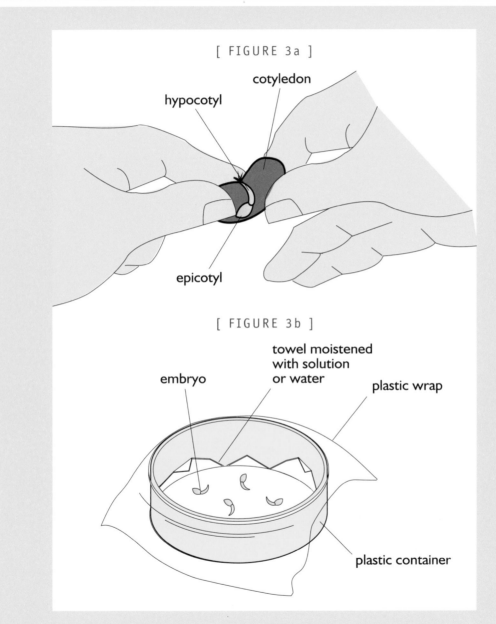

[FIGURE 3a]

cotyledon

hypocotyl

epicotyl

[FIGURE 3b]

embryo

towel moistened
with solution
or water

plastic wrap

plastic container

3 a) To remove a bean embryo from its cotyledons, push it gently
with your thumb. b) Place the embryos on moist paper towels in
a container and cover it with plastic wrap.

Bean seeds use the food stored in their cotyledons to germinate and grow. But suppose a bean seed loses its cotyledons. Can it still grow?

The answer may be that it can grow if we supply a substitute for the food that was stored in the cotyledons. To test that idea, soak about three dozen lima bean seeds overnight. Then prepare a solution by dissolving a teaspoon of sugar in a plastic cup (6–8 oz) nearly filled with water. In the same way, prepare a solution of salt and another of honey. Fill two additional cups with plain water. Label the cups.

Next, fold paper towels to fit on the bottoms of five wide, plastic containers. Label them the same way you labeled the cups. Pour enough of the sugar solution over the towel in the dish labeled "sugar" to make it moist. Keep the remaining solution to moisten the towel as it becomes drier. A small piece of cardboard or plastic can be used to cover the solution in the cup. Place the labeled cup next to the container with the towels and seeds so you will be sure you have the right dishes and cups together.

Repeat the procedure for the honey and salt solutions. Sprinkle some starch on the fourth towel (starch is not soluble in water) and then add enough water to moisten the towel. To the last towel add plain water.

Now that the moist towels are in place, you are ready to work on the seeds. Take one bean seed and peel away the seed coat. Then gently slide one cotyledon off the other. You can now see the embryo resting on the remaining cotyledon. To isolate the embryo, place your thumb at the embryo's center as shown in Figure 3a. Push gently to free the embryo. Don't be discouraged if you don't succeed on your first try. With a little practice you will be able to separate the embryos easily.

As you isolate the embryos, place them on the towels that contain the five different liquids (sugar, honey, salt, starch, and water). Try to get at least five embryos on each towel.

Cover the containers that hold the embryos and damp towels with clear plastic wrap (see Figure 3b). Don't seal the wrap. It should be loose enough for air to reach the embryos. In addition to retarding

evaporation, the clear plastic wrap will allow diffuse light (not bright sunlight) to reach the embryos.

On which, if any, of the towels do the embryos continue to grow? Which liquids seem to meet the nutritional needs of the growing embryos? For how long do the embryos continue to grow?

Science Fair Project Idea

Plant scientists can grow mature plants from embryos like the ones you placed on different solutions. What do you think they have to do to make this happen? Repeat this experiment by using just the solutions on which the embryos grow well and carefully planting the embryos in soil after they have grown on the solutions for some time. Do you think the embryo plants will continue to grow after being transplanted to soil? Do they?

Materials:

- 4 large flowerpots
- potting soil
- sand
- peat
- gravel
- 20 bean seeds
- water
- measuring cup
- ruler

Does the type of soil in which seeds are planted affect their germination? To find out, fill flowerpots with different kinds of soil. Put potting soil in one pot, sand in a second, peat in a third, and gravel in a fourth. Plant five bean seeds about 1 cm (0.5 in) deep in each pot. Keep the soils damp but not wet. Put all the pots together in a warm, sunny spot.

In which soils do the seeds germinate? In which soil do the seeds germinate first?

In those soils where seeds germinate, continue to water the growing plants with equal amounts of water. In which soils do the seedlings grow into mature plants?

Measure the heights and count the leaves on the plants in the various soils every other day until they mature (produce flowers). Record your data in your science notebook. Compare the growth rates and the number of leaves on the plants in the different soils. In which soils do the plants thrive? In which soils do the plants die or grow poorly?

Science Fair Project Idea

Try a variety of soils and soil mixtures other than those you tried in this experiment. How do those soils affect germination and plant growth?

1.5 How Does a Turntable Affect Growing Grass?

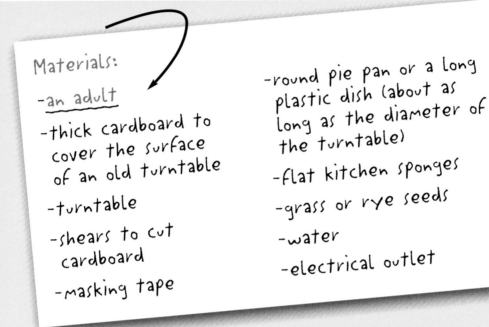

Materials:

- an adult
- thick cardboard to cover the surface of an old turntable
- turntable
- shears to cut cardboard
- masking tape
- round pie pan or a long plastic dish (about as long as the diameter of the turntable)
- flat kitchen sponges
- grass or rye seeds
- water
- electrical outlet

When you ride your bike around a curve, you feel a force that seems to be pushing you outward. We call this a *centrifugal force*. You compensate for this force by leaning inward. You feel a similar force on a merry-go-round or a playground whirligig. Plants, of course, would experience the same force if they were growing on a merry-go-round. To see how they react to such a force, you can grow some grass or rye on a spinning turntable. The seedlings will "feel" a force that seems to be pushing them outward.

As you know from other experiments, roots grow downward and stems grow upward regardless of how the seeds are planted. Stems grow in a direction that opposes gravity, and roots grow in the direction that gravity pulls them. Can you guess how plants will grow on a spinning turntable?

To find out if you are right, **ask an adult** to cut a piece of thick cardboard so that it fits on the top of an old turntable and use masking tape to hold the cardboard in place. Cover the bottom of a large, round pie pan or a long plastic dish (about as long as the diameter of the turntable) with flat kitchen sponges. You may have to cut some of the sponges so they fill the space within the pie pan or dish. Add water to the sponges and then sprinkle grass or rye seeds on them.

Put the pan of seeds you planted on the turntable in a well-lighted location. **Make sure your hands are dry and then turn on the turntable on its lowest speed.** The seeds will spin as they germinate and grow. Keep the sponges damp but not wet by occasionally adding water.

How do the seedlings grow after they germinate? Do they grow straight up? Do they grow leaning toward the center of the turntable? Or do they grow outward leaning away from the center of the turntable?

What evidence do you have that plants respond to centrifugal forces? Do they respond in the same way that you do when you experience a centrifugal force? What evidence do you have that the centrifugal force grows larger as the distance from the center of the turntable increases?

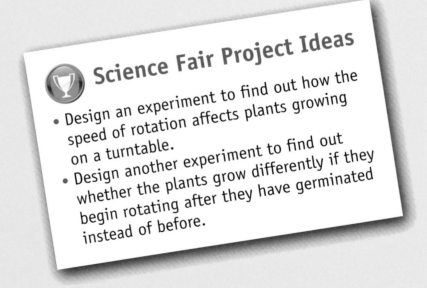

Science Fair Project Ideas

- Design an experiment to find out how the speed of rotation affects plants growing on a turntable.
- Design another experiment to find out whether the plants grow differently if they begin rotating after they have germinated instead of before.

1.6 Growing a Dandelion Plant from Seed

Materials:
- lint from clothes dryer, or paper towels
- plastic box with clear cover
- water
- dandelion seed puff

Plants reproduce in many different ways. The most familiar form of plant reproduction is from a seed, and few seeds are more common than those of the dandelion (see Figure 4). How does a plant such as a dandelion grow from an airborne seed?

To prepare your "seed bed," gather lint from a clothes dryer and cover the bottom of a plastic box with it. Sprinkle it with water. (If clothes dryer lint is not available to you, use paper towels instead.)

After a dandelion plant produces flowers, it shrivels and stays closed until it opens to become a white seed puff. Find a dandelion that has a white seed puff. Hold the seed puff above your prepared seed bed and gently blow so that the seeds become airborne and land inside the box.

Put the cover on the box and place the box in a sunny spot. Observe your seed bed each day. The dandelion seeds will detach themselves from their parachutes and develop into seedlings. Observe your seedlings as they grow, and be sure to keep the lint or paper towels moist. Write your observations in your science notebook, noting the time and date and a description of what you see.

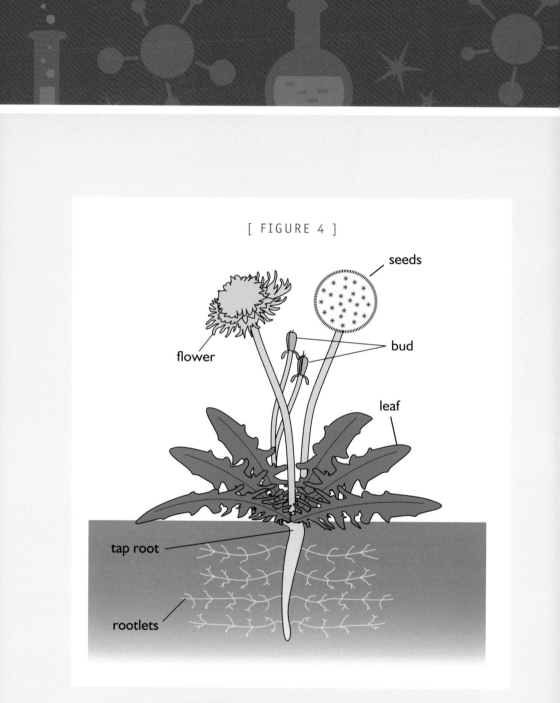

[FIGURE 4]

seeds

flower

bud

leaf

tap root

rootlets

A dandelion plant has airborne seeds.

Science Fair Project Ideas

- Dandelions are common and very adaptable plants. Look at dandelions that you find growing in different places. In a field of uncut grass, the dandelion will have a long stalk. In a lawn where the grass has been cut, the dandelion grows with a short flower stalk, and the leaves spread out flat. What other plants adapt and change when growing in different places?

- Maple seeds are shaped like helicopter propellers. Try sprouting some maple seeds on damp paper towels. What happens to the parts of the seed?

Chapter 2

Leaves

IN THE LAST CHAPTER, YOU SAW THAT A VARIETY OF FACTORS AFFECT THE GERMINATION OF SEEDS. You learned that seeds contain nutrients that provide energy for germination and the initial growth of the plant. Once the plant sends a stem and leaves upward, it can begin using sunlight to make its own food. Leaves are the food factories for virtually all living things. Food (in the form of sugars) is made using a process called *photosynthesis*.

Sunlight energy is required for plants to carry out photosynthesis. Plants take in carbon dioxide and water and produce sugar and oxygen. The broad, flat surface of leaves is well-adapted for absorbing sunlight's energy. Leaves also contain a green pigment called chlorophyll that is needed in photosynthesis. You have probably noticed lines or veins in leaves. What do you think veins do? Leaves also have microscopic holes called *stomata* in them. What might holes in the leaves do?

In this chapter, you will learn about leaves and their structure. You will investigate the effect of light and dark on plant leaves. You will collect data to demonstrate that photosynthesis is happening by testing for the presence of sugars and production of carbon dioxide. Finally, you will use a lab technique called *chromatography* to separate pigments found in leaves.

2.1 How Does Light Affect Leaves?

Materials:
- small potted plant
- south-facing window
- water

Place a small potted plant near a south-facing window where the sun shines in most of the day. Be sure that the plant's leaves face all directions evenly or are turned predominantly toward the inside of the room. Water the plant so that the soil in which it is growing remains damp but not wet.

Watch the plant carefully over a period of several weeks. What happens to the leaves? How does their orientation change? Do they tend to turn so that they face the light? What does this tell you about the leaves?

Can you develop a hypothesis to explain why the leaves turn as they do? Can you design an experiment that will test your hypothesis?

2.2 Leaves and Veins

Materials:
-a variety of plants that have different leaves
-paper and pencil

If you look at leaves closely, you will see lines running through them (see Figure 5a, which shows a typical leaf). Feel the lines, and you will find that they are quite hard. They are called veins. As you can see, the veins all connect with the leaf's stem or *petiole*. The petiole is the part that connects the leaf's wide blade with the stem of the plant. Some leaves with different vein structures are shown in Figure 5. The veins, which lead to small branches and eventually to the main stem and roots, carry water and minerals to the cells that make up the leaf. The veins also provide a skeleton to support leaves and make them stiff. A floppy leaf would not offer much surface area to the light that the leaves need to manufacture food.

The way the veins are arranged (the venation) varies, but it is usually either parallel or netted. Leaves with netted venation have veins that branch off one another in various ways. Netted venation may be palmate or pinnate. In palmate venation, which is characteristic of maple and sycamore leaves, several main veins branch off the petiole like the fingers on a hand (Figure 5b). Leaves with pinnate venation, such as elm and wild cherry, have one main vein from which a number of side branches arise (Figure 5c). In parallel venation the veins run lengthwise along the leaf and are parallel to one another (Figure 5d). Such venation is characteristic of corn, iris, wheat, and grasses. Netlike venation is commonly found in plants with seeds that have two cotyledons (dicots), while parallel venation is common among monocots (plants whose seeds have a single cotyledon).

Look at the leaves you find on various plants. Draw the leaves and the vein patterns within the leaves. Which plants have leaves with parallel veins? Which plants have leaves with netted venation? Which leaves

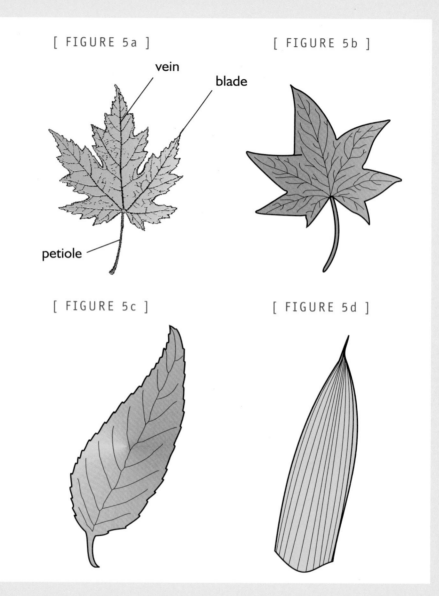

[FIGURE 5a]

vein

blade

petiole

[FIGURE 5b]

[FIGURE 5c]

[FIGURE 5d]

5 a) A typical leaf showing petiole, blade, and veins. b) A sweetgum leaf is an example of palmate venation. c) This wild cherry leaf is an example of pinnate venation. d) Corn leaves like this one illustrate parallel venation.

have palmate venation? Which have pinnate venation? What other differences do you notice as you compare the leaves of different plants?

Does the venation of the leaves on trees have any relationship to the structure of the bark? Is venation related to the color the leaves turn in autumn?

Materials:

- an adult
- paper clip
- black construction paper or aluminum foil
- geranium plant
- gloves
- safety glasses
- tongs
- stove
- pot of boiling water
- alcohol
- small jar
- saucer
- tincture of iodine
- measuring teaspoon
- water

Leaves are green because they contain pigments that absorb most of the colors in white light except green. Because green light is reflected instead of being absorbed, most leaves appear green. One of the pigments in the cells of a plant's leaves is chlorophyll. Chlorophyll absorbs the light that provides the energy plants need to carry on photosynthesis.

Photosynthesis is a process involving many steps by which plants convert carbon dioxide and water to oxygen and sugar. The oxygen that most living things need to carry on *respiration* (the release of energy from food) is produced during the process of photosynthesis.

Because excess sugar produced in a leaf is changed to starch and stored, you can use the common test for starch (iodine) to confirm that food is produced in leaves when light is present. To carry out this test, begin by using a paper clip to hold a small folded piece of black construction paper or aluminum foil over both sides of a geranium leaf as shown in Figure 6. Be careful not to damage the leaf when you attach the paper.

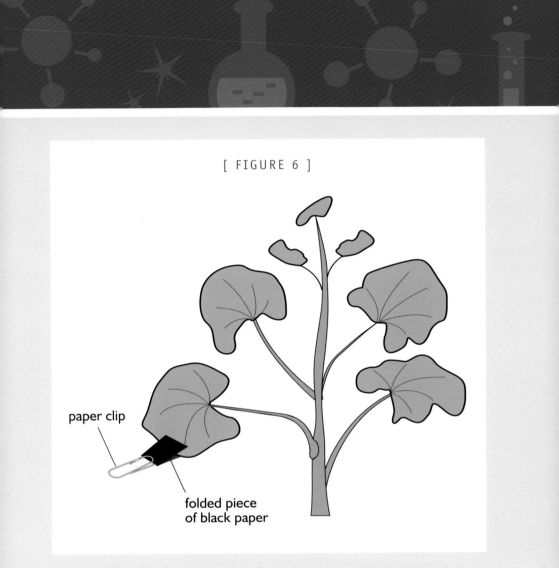

[FIGURE 6]

paper clip

folded piece
of black paper

Use a paper clip to fasten a piece of black construction paper to a
geranium leaf. Light will not be able to reach the leaf cells covered
by the paper, but it will reach the other cells in the leaf.

Do this in the morning on a bright sunny day when lots of light will fall
on the leaves of the geranium plant.

After four or five hours, pick the leaf from the plant, bring it indoors,
and remove the paper or foil. Under adult supervision, and while
wearing gloves and safety glasses, use tongs to hold the leaf's stem so
that you can immerse the rest of the leaf into a pot of boiling water.

on a stove. Hold the leaf under the boiling water for about one minute. The heat will break open cell walls within the leaf. Turn off the stove. Let the hot water cool before discarding it.

Next, you need to extract the green chlorophyll from the leaf. To do this, place the now limp leaf in a small jar of alcohol and leave it overnight. **(Caution: Because alcohol is flammable, never let it get near a flame or red-hot burner.)**

The next morning you will find that the alcohol has a green color due to the pigments it has extracted from the leaf.

In a saucer, mix together approximately equal amounts of tincture of iodine solution and water: about 5 ml (1 teaspoon) of each will do. **Remember: Iodine is poisonous. Handle it carefully! Do not put it in your mouth.** Next, rinse the leaf in warm water before you spread it out and place it in the iodine–water solution.

You will see the leaf turn color as the iodine reacts with the starch to form a dark blue-black color. Notice that one area of the leaf is much lighter than the rest. Can you identify that region? In which area of the leaf did photosynthesis not take place? How can you tell? What evidence do you have to show that light is required for photosynthesis?

Science Fair Project Idea

Design and carry out an experiment to determine how long the starch produced in bright light remains in the leaf after the leaf is placed in a dark place.

2.4 Do Plants Produce Carbon Dioxide?

Materials:

- 4 test tubes
- water
- masking tape
- marking pen
- bromthymol blue solution (borrowed from a science teacher)
- dropper
- drinking straw
- sprigs of elodea (or other pond plant)
- 4 rubber stoppers that fit test tubes
- 4 glasses or beakers
- lightbulb

During photosynthesis plants combine carbon dioxide and water in the presence of light to produce food and oxygen. The food is either stored by the plant or used as an energy source. (Plants, like you, use food as a source of energy.) The process by which energy is obtained from food is called *respiration*. During respiration, food is oxidized; that is, the food combines with oxygen in a complicated series of chemical reactions. The end products of respiration are carbon dioxide and water, the very same chemicals that are combined to make food during photosynthesis. But only green plants can manufacture food, and they can do so only in the presence of light.

With all this information in mind, fill four test tubes about halfway with water. Place a small piece of masking tape on each tube and label them 1, 2, 3, and 4. Add a few drops of bromthymol blue to each tube. Bromthymol blue is an acid-base indicator. It is blue in a base, such as

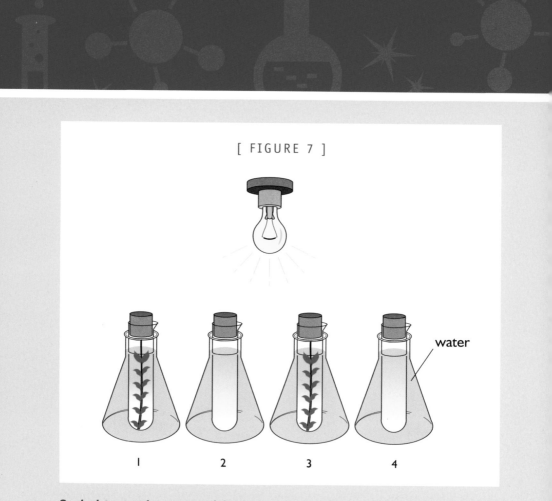

[FIGURE 7]

water

1   2   3   4

Sealed test tubes, two with elodea plants, are placed in containers of water near a light source.

ammonia, and yellow in an acid, such as vinegar or a solution of carbon dioxide. Carbon dioxide forms carbonic acid when it dissolves in water.

Using a drinking straw, gently blow air from your lungs into tubes 1 and 2. **(Be careful not to get the water in your mouth.)** Continue to blow in air until no further change occurs. How can you explain the fact that the solutions turn from blue to yellow?

Place sprigs of elodea (or other pond plant) in tubes 1 and 3. (Elodea is a water plant commonly found in ponds or in stores that sell aquarium supplies.) Seal the openings of all four test tubes with rubber stoppers. Place the tubes in glasses or beakers of water near a bright light source as shown in Figure 7. Be sure the tubes are not so close to the light that the water becomes hot. After several hours, record any changes you see. Continue to watch the tubes for an entire day. What changes occur?

What is the purpose of each of the four tubes in this investigation? What do the changes in each tube indicate?

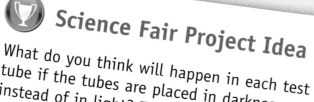

🏆 **Science Fair Project Idea**

What do you think will happen in each test tube if the tubes are placed in darkness instead of in light? Test your predictions by repeating the experiment with the plants in darkness.

2.5 How Does Darkness Affect Plants?

Materials:

- shears
- sponge
- 2 saucers
- grass seed
- water
- window or light source
- dark area, such as a closet or box
- board
- green grass

Will plants produce chlorophyll in the absence of light? You can find out by germinating grass seeds in light and in darkness.

Begin by cutting a sponge in half. Place each half on a separate saucer. Sprinkle grass seed over each sponge. Then add water to the saucers so that it is about halfway up the sides of the sponges. Leave one saucer and sponge near a window or a light. Put the other saucer in a closet or under a box so that the seeds will be in darkness. Check each day to be sure that there is water in the saucers.

How much time passes before the seeds begin to germinate? Continue to add water to the saucers and watch the seeds. Do seeds germinate in both places? If they do, what is different about the two sets of germinated seedlings? Does chlorophyll develop in grass seedlings that receive no light? How do you know?

Here is another way to find out if light is needed for grass to produce chlorophyll. Place a board on some green grass near the edge of a field. (Obtain permission from the owner before you do so.) Leave the board in place, but look under it every few days until you can draw a conclusion based on what you observe. What happens to the grass under the board? What did you conclude? Remove the board when the experiment is finished.

Materials:

- beet leaves
- mortar and pestle, or old pie pan and rock
- measuring tablespoon
- small amount of white sand
- rubbing alcohol
- cotton swab
- white, cone-shaped coffee filter
- narrow glass jar
- ruler

Many trees shed their leaves in the fall. Dropping leaves prevents water loss through the winter. As autumn approaches, trees stop producing chlorophyll, which is a green pigment that is used in photosynthesis. At that time of year, when the green pigment fades, other colors in the leaf can be seen.

You can find these other colors (or pigments) in leaves before autumn approaches. Take fresh beet leaves. They can come from a home garden, or you may be able to buy a bunch of beets with the leaves still attached. You may need to ask the produce manager of the grocery store for help, because sometimes clerks remove the leaves before putting the beets out for sale.

Tear four or five beet leaves into small pieces and put them in an old pie pan. When you have a pile of torn pieces of leaves, add a small quantity (about one tablespoonful) of white sand for grit. Add about two tablespoons of rubbing alcohol. Using a rock, grind up the leaves. (You can use a mortar and pestle if you have them.)

Continue grinding the leaves together with the rubbing alcohol and sand until you have ground them into a dark green liquid. Use a cotton swab to paint a spot of this dark green liquid on a white coffee-filter cone, about halfway up the side of the filter. Put on two dozen coats of the green liquid, letting the spot dry between each coat.

Put about 2 cm (1 in) of rubbing alcohol into a narrow glass jar. Place the coffee filter into the jar and submerge the tip in the rubbing alcohol. Be sure that the alcohol is not deep enough to reach the spot that you have painted on the side of the filter. After ten minutes, remove the cone from the jar and spread it out on the table.

What colors do you see? Note the time, date, and species of leaf along with your observations in your science notebook.

Chromatography is used to separate and identify mixtures of chemical compounds. This experiment makes use of paper chromatography. The colored chemicals (pigments) from the ground leaves are dissolved by the alcohol and carried in the alcohol up through the cone. Some of the chemicals are less soluble in the alcohol than others. They stay put or move only a short distance, while those more soluble in alcohol move farther. As different colored chemicals are left behind, colored bands form. Each band is a different pigment.

🏆 Science Fair Project Idea

Repeat this experiment using different kinds of leaves or using leaves collected at different times of the year. What results would you get using spinach leaves?

2.7 What Is Transpiration?

Materials:

- small jar
- water
- cardboard
- clear plastic cup
- nail
- petroleum jelly
- small leaf from a shade tree, such as a maple
- stone

You've probably noticed the broad, flat surface of leaves and the veins running through them. But have you ever seen microscopic holes, called *stomata* or *stomates*, on the surface of leaves? When the leaves become warm, tiny drops of water escape through the stomata into the air as water vapor. This process is called *transpiration*.

Transpiration is the loss of water from a plant. It occurs primarily through the leaves where the stomates provide easy access to the air surrounding the plant. To see evidence of transpiration, gather a small jar nearly filled with water, a square piece of cardboard large enough to cover the mouth of the jar, a clear plastic cup, a nail, and some petroleum jelly. Use the nail to make a small hole in the center of the cardboard. Carefully remove a small but healthy leaf from a shade tree, such as a maple. Be sure to include the entire stem (petiole) of the leaf. Place the leaf's stem through the hole in the cardboard. Then put the cardboard on the mouth of the jar so that the lower end of the leaf's petiole is in the water as shown in Figure 8.

Spread a thick layer of petroleum jelly around the rim of the plastic cup and around the leaf's stem at the point where it passes through the cardboard. Then invert the cup over the leaf. The petroleum jelly will form a seal around the mouth of the cup and the leaf's stem so that gases can't enter or leave the cup through its mouth or through the hole in the cardboard.

LEAVES **43**

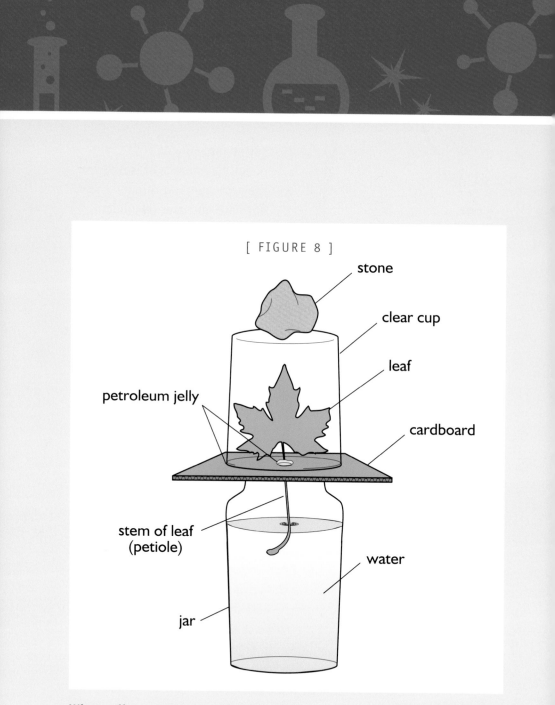

[FIGURE 8]

stone

clear cup

leaf

petroleum jelly

cardboard

stem of leaf
(petiole)

water

jar

What collects on the inside surface of the cup during the experiment?

Put the apparatus you have assembled in a sunny place. If there is a breeze, place a stone on the bottom of the cup to prevent it from moving. After an hour or two, look at the cup. What do you see collecting on the inside of the inverted cup that covers the leaf? How could it have gotten there? What do you think it is? What test could you perform to be sure?

Science Fair Project Idea

Design and carry out an experiment to show that the water transpired from a plant's leaves is the same water that entered the plant through its roots.

Materials:

- 5 small coleus plants
- shears
- warm, sunny day
- water
- 5 clear plastic sandwich bags
- 5 twist ties
- petroleum jelly
- balance (preferably top-loading)
- warm, dark place
- electric fan
- notebook and pencil

Obtain a flat of small coleus plants. The plants are probably in small plastic containers that are joined together. Use shears to cut through the plastic that joins the tops of the containers in which the plants are growing. Pick five of the plants that appear to be very similar in size and number of leaves and begin this experiment on the morning of a bright, warm, sunny day.

Water the soil in which the plants are growing. Slip a plastic sandwich bag over the container that holds the soil for each plant as shown in Figure 9a. Use a twist tie to seal the top of the bag around the stem of each plant. Cover the top sides of the leaves of one plant with petroleum jelly. Cover the lower sides of the leaves of a second plant with petroleum jelly.

Weigh each of the plants on a balance (Figure 9b) and record their masses in grams in a table similar to Table 1. Place the two plants with petroleum jelly in warm sunlight (Figure 9c). Place one of the three remaining plants, which will serve as a control in this experiment, in the same place. Place a second in sunlight, but use an electric fan to

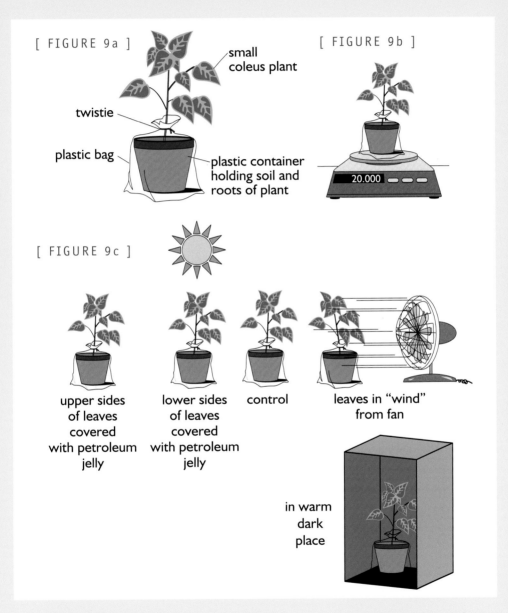

[FIGURE 9a]

small coleus plant

twistie

plastic bag

plastic container holding soil and roots of plant

[FIGURE 9b]

20.000

[FIGURE 9c]

upper sides of leaves covered with petroleum jelly

lower sides of leaves covered with petroleum jelly

control

leaves in "wind" from fan

in warm dark place

9 a) Select five small coleus plants. Seal the pots with plastic bags, as shown. b) Weigh each plant and record the data. c) After preparing the plants in different ways, place four of them in sunlight and one in darkness.

TABLE 1.
Mass of Plants Under Different Conditions

Plant	Conditions	Mass in grams after						Mass in grams next morning
		0 h	2 h	4 h	6 h	8 h	10 h	
1	Tops of leaves coated							
2	Bottom sides coated							
3	Control							
4	In wind							
5	Kept in dark							

provide a constant breeze (air flow) over the plant. Place the third remaining plant in a warm, dark place.

Reweigh each plant at two-hour intervals throughout the rest of the day. Between weighings return each plant to its assigned place.

At the end of the day, leave the plants in place overnight. Early the next morning make a final weighing of each one.

Which plant lost the most water through its leaves during the day? Which plant lost the least amount of water during the day? Two plants had their leaves coated with petroleum jelly, one on the upper sides of the leaves, the other on the lower sides. Based on the water losses of these two plants, are there more stomates on the lower or upper sides of leaves? What evidence do you have to support your conclusion?

What did you learn about the effect of light on the rate at which transpiration takes place? What effect does wind have on transpiration? How do you know?

Science Fair Project Idea

What other factors might affect transpiration? Do you think temperature or humidity affect transpiration? Design an experiment to investigate.

Chapter 3

Stems, Roots, and Buds

STEMS, ROOTS, AND BUDS PLAY VITAL ROLES IN NORMAL PLANT GROWTH. The stem develops from the epicotyl of the seed's embryo. The stem transports water and minerals to the leaves and other tissues. It also provides support for the plant. A plant's primary root develops from the embryo's radicle (tip of the hypocotyl), which puts out secondary roots. The roots take up water and dissolved minerals from the soil. You've probably seen leaf buds on twigs or branches. Buds are undeveloped leaves that are in a resting state. They often have a scaly covering for protection. When conditions are right, buds develop into leaves.

In this chapter, you will learn more about stems, roots, and buds. You will look at how they grow and what they do. You will also investigate the effect of factors such as gravity and light on their development and function.

Materials:

- -2 small coleus plants
- -sunny place
- -brick or block of wood
- -warm dark place, such as a closet
- -cardboard sheets
- -blocks
- -tape

Place two small coleus plants side by side in a sunny place. Be sure the soil is damp and firmly tamped down. Then turn one of the plants on its side so it is horizontally rather than vertically oriented, as shown in Figure 10. Use a brick or a block of wood to keep the plant above the ground, floor, or table. Watch the two plants over the course of a day or two. What happens to the plant that is turned on its side? Does it continue to grow horizontally or does its stem turn upward?

Do you think the plant turned as it did because of its response to gravity or because of its response to light? You can find out by placing the same two plants in a warm, dark place for a day or two. This time turn the other plant so it is horizontally oriented. Place the plant you turned before in a vertical position.

Does the horizontal plant remain oriented in that direction or does its stem turn upward? Based on your observations in these two experiments, do you think the stem turned because of its response to gravity or to light?

Do coleus plants always grow in a direction that opposes gravity regardless of the angle they are turned relative to "up"? To find out, repeat the experiment you just did, but this time use cardboard sheets, blocks, and tape to build inclines that allow you to tip the plants at various angles, such as the ones shown in Figure 11.

To avoid any attraction toward light, place the plants in a dark place. After several days in the dark, are all the plants growing in the direction opposite from gravity's pull? When turned back with their pots on a level surface, will these crooked plants return to their former upward growth?

[FIGURE 10]

vertical plant

horizontal plant

What happens to a plant when it is turned on its side?

[FIGURE 11]

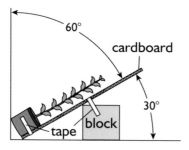

Plant tipped 60° from normal

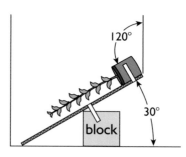

Plant tipped 120° from normal

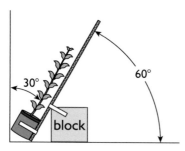

Plant tipped 30° from normal

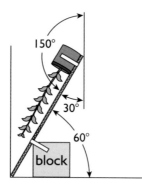

Plant tipped 150° from normal

Will coleus plants always grow opposing gravity regardless of the amount they are tipped?

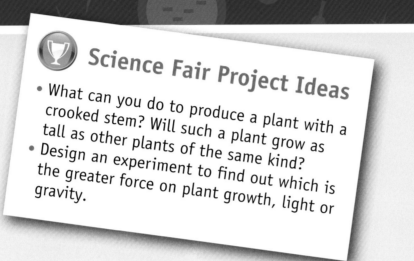

Science Fair Project Ideas

- What can you do to produce a plant with a crooked stem? Will such a plant grow as tall as other plants of the same kind?
- Design an experiment to find out which is the greater force on plant growth, light or gravity.

Materials:

-an adult

-2 fresh stalks
of celery

-bowl or basin

-water

-sharp knife

-2 drinking glasses

-cooking syringe
(baster)

-red food coloring

-cutting board

-magnifying glass

Water is absorbed through the roots of a plant. To reach the leaves, it must pass upward through the stem. Once in the leaves, water is used to make food, but much of it is lost through transpiration, the loss of water vapor.

To see the path followed by water in its upward movement through a plant, you need two fresh celery stalks with leaves. One of the stalks will serve as a control. Place this stalk in a bowl or basin of water. Have an adult use a sharp knife to cut away the lowermost part of the stalk while it is under water. The cutting should be done under water so that air bubbles cannot enter the stem. If they do, they break the column of water that moves from stem to leaves. Next, put a drinking glass in the bowl or basin and transfer the celery stalk under water into the glass.

Repeat the experiment with a second stalk of celery. Use a kitchen syringe (baster) to remove all but about 3 to 4 cm (1.25 to 1.75 in) of water from both glasses. To the water surrounding the second stalk, add enough red food coloring to make the water very dark. Leave the stalks for several hours. Check periodically until you see evidence of the red food coloring in the veins of the celery leaves (Figure 12). While the

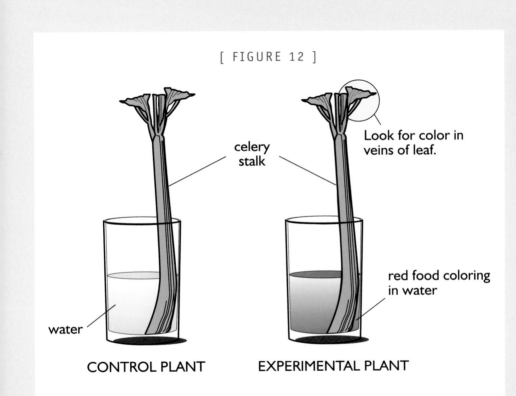

[FIGURE 12]

celery
stalk

Look for color in
veins of leaf.

red food coloring
in water

water

CONTROL PLANT

EXPERIMENTAL PLANT

Celery stalks can be used to detect the upward movement of water in the
stem of a plant.

veins may not appear to be distinctly red, they will be noticeably different from those in the control where colorless water was used.

Once you have detected the presence of food coloring in the veins of the experimental stalk, remove the stalk from the water and place it on a cutting board. Have an adult use the sharp knife to cut the stalk about 3 cm (1.25 in) above its lower end. Can you see where the red food coloring has moved up the stem?

Continue to cut the stem at 3-cm intervals. Can you follow the path of the colored water up the stem? Continue to cut all the way to the leaves. Can you find evidence showing that the colored water entered the short stems (petioles) leading to the leaves? Using a magnifying lens, can you find evidence that the colored water entered the veins of the leaves?

You can apply what you have learned by making a "Fourth of July" bouquet. To make the bouquet, find some white, long-stemmed flowers commonly known as Queen Anne's lace. Pick six of them, cut the lower ends of their stems under water, and place two of them in a glass containing water to which red food coloring has been added. Place two more in a glass containing water to which blue food coloring has been added. Place the remaining two in a glass of plain water. Wait a few hours and you will have your "Fourth of July" bouquet.

Can you make a Queen Anne's lace flower that has red, white, and blue colors all in the same blossom? Can you make a Queen Anne's bouquet that would be appropriate for St. Patrick's Day?

Materials:

- bean seeds
- flowerpot
- potting or garden soil
- ruler
- fine-line permanent marker

Plant several bean seeds in a flowerpot that is nearly filled with soil. After the seeds have germinated and a young plant with leaves growing outward from several points (nodes) along the stem has emerged, choose one of the plants to study. Using a ruler and a fine-line permanent marker, carefully mark the entire stem with fine lines 2 mm apart as shown in Figure 13. At two-day intervals, remeasure the distance between the lines. Continue to do this for at least two weeks.

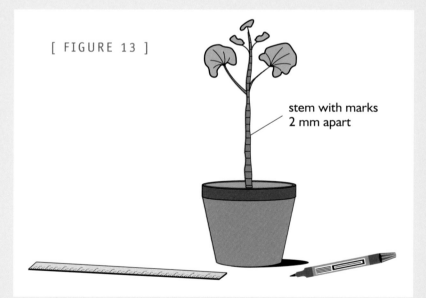

[FIGURE 13]

stem with marks 2 mm apart

By marking a stem at 2-mm intervals, you can find out where a stem grows.

On the basis of your measurements, what can you conclude? Where does growth take place in a stem? What additional evidence do you have to support your conclusion? If you hang a swing from the limb of a tree, does the height of the swing's seat from the ground change with time? If it does, how does it change?

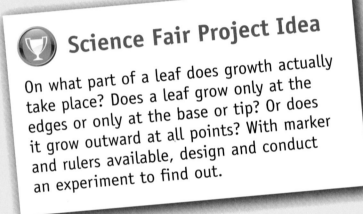

Science Fair Project Idea

On what part of a leaf does growth actually take place? Does a leaf grow only at the edges or only at the base or tip? Or does it grow outward at all points? With marker and rulers available, design and conduct an experiment to find out.

Materials:

- 20 corn seeds
- cup
- water
- paper towels
- wide, shallow pan
- plastic wrap
- ruler
- fine-line permanent marker
- clear plastic tape
- thin stick
- 250-mL (1/2 pint) beaker
- warm place
- measuring cup

Soak about twenty corn seeds in a cup of water overnight. Then place the seeds on some moist paper towels folded to fit on the bottom of a wide, shallow pan. Cover the pan with plastic wrap and keep the towels moist, not wet, until all the seeds have germinated.

From the germinated corn seedlings, choose one with a root that is about 2 to 3 cm (1.0 to 1.25 in) long. (You can use the other seeds in Experiment 3.5, which you may also start at this time.) Use a ruler and a permanent marker to draw lines 2 mm apart on the root. Use a piece of clear plastic tape to attach the seedling to a thin stick. Place the stick inside a small (250-ml or half-pint) beaker or jar that has about 50 ml (2 oz) of water on the bottom as shown in Figure 14. Be sure the root does not touch the water.

Put the beaker or jar in a warm, not hot, place. After three to four days, remove the seedling and remeasure the distance between the lines you drew on the root.

On the basis of your measurements, what can you conclude? Where does growth take place in a root?

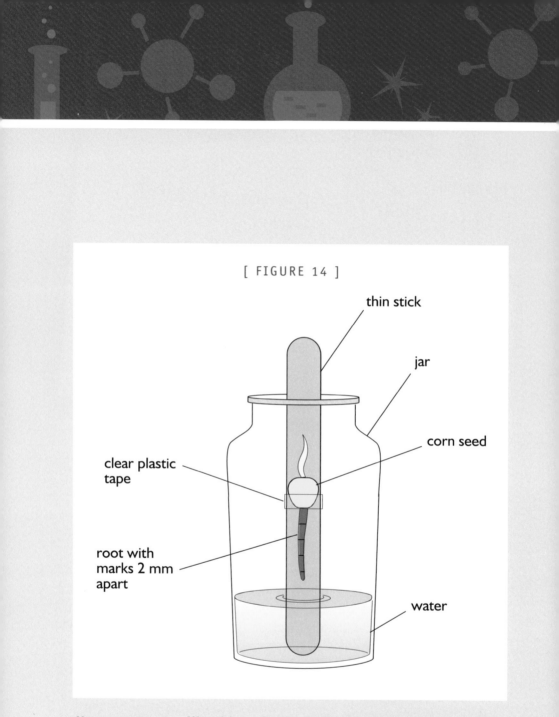

[FIGURE 14]

thin stick

jar

corn seed

clear plastic tape

root with marks 2 mm apart

water

Use an apparatus like this to find out where growth occurs in a root.

Science Fair Project Idea

Repeat the experiment with other seeds, such as bean and squash seeds. Is the growth pattern of their roots the same as it was for the roots of corn seeds?

Materials:

-an adult

-12 germinated corn seeds

-ruler

-sharp knife

-clear glass or plastic container

-moist sand

-masking tape

-marking pen

-water

From the seeds you germinated for the preceding experiment, select 12 with roots about 3 cm (1.25 in) long. **Have an adult** use a sharp knife to remove 2 mm from the tip of the roots of 6 of these seedlings. The roots of the other 6 seedlings, which will serve as controls, should not be cut.

Half-fill a clear glass or plastic container with moist sand. On one side of the container, gently insert the 6 seedlings, whose root tips have been removed, between the sand and the clear wall. The roots should be horizontal (see Figure 15). Insert the 6 controls in a similar manner on the other side of the container. Then fill the container with moist sand. Use masking tape and a marking pen to label the controls and experimental seedlings.

Observe both sets of seedlings over a period of a week. Add water if necessary to keep the sand moist. Do the roots that have had their tips removed continue to grow? What about the controls? Does the direction of growth of the cut roots change? What about the controls? What can you conclude from the results of your experiment?

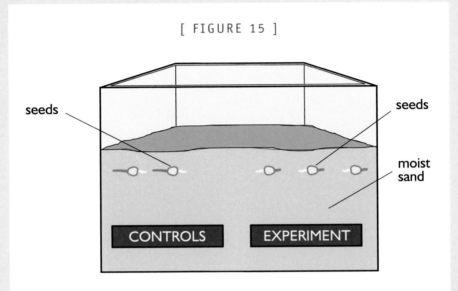

[FIGURE 15]

What happens to a corn seed if you cut off the tip of its root?

🏆 Science Fair Project Idea

Repeat the experiment using other seeds, such as bean and squash seeds. Are the results the same as they were for corn seeds?

Materials:

- an adult

- deciduous trees, especially maples, horse chestnuts, and willows

- sharp pruning clippers

- field guide for trees and bushes

- marking pen

- masking tape

- tweezers (forceps)

- magnifying glass (convex lens)

- ruler

- sink

- containers to hold and support twigs

- water

- warm, sunny place

Deciduous trees shed their leaves in the fall (when the hours of daylight diminish) and spend part of the year without their green "coats." Despite their naked look, these plants have new leaves ready and waiting for the onset of longer days. The new leaves are inside buds. Find buds like the ones shown in Figure 16. To study the buds more closely, collect twigs from a variety of trees. Be sure to ask permission from whoever owns the trees before you do so.

Under adult supervision, cut the twigs with pruning clippers. A field guide (book) for trees and bushes will help you identify any plants that you don't recognize without their leaves. Cut several small twigs from each kind of tree. Use a marking pen to write the name of the tree on a piece of masking tape. Wrap the label around the twig so that you can identify it later.

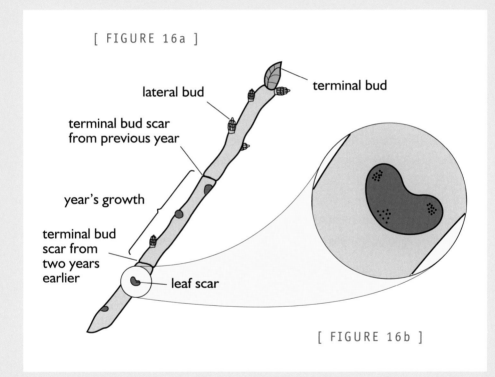

[FIGURE 16a]

terminal bud

lateral bud

terminal bud scar
from previous year

year's growth

terminal bud
scar from
two years
earlier

leaf scar

[FIGURE 16b]

16 a) A twig is shown with its buds and its leaf and terminal bud scars.
   b) The drawing shows an enlarged leaf scar.

Once you have gathered and identified some twigs, take them indoors to examine them more closely. With a pair of tweezers (forceps), peel away some of the brown scales from a *terminal bud* (one at the end of a twig). You should be able to see tiny leaves inside. Use a magnifying glass (convex lens) to examine the buds and baby leaves more closely. Can you find terminal buds (Figure 16a)? Can you find lateral buds? The distance between terminal bud scars is the growth that occurs from one year to the next. How much did each twig grow during the past year?

Return to the trees from which you cut the twigs. Look closely at the terminal buds on their twigs and branches. How much does growth vary from year to year? Can you find evidence of a recent drought?

Use the magnifier to look at the leaf scars (Figure 16b) on the sides of the twigs. The scars were made when leaves that grew from the twig during previous years fell off. Notice the small dots within each scar. The dots reveal where vessels that carried water, food, and minerals up from the roots and through the stem entered the leaf's petiole (stem). Some of these scars, especially the ones on horse chestnut trees, look like faces.

Ask an adult to fill a sink with water and cut off the lower 3 cm (1.25 in) of the twigs under water so that air doesn't enter the vessels in the stems. Place a vase or other vessel under the water and insert the cut ends of the twigs. Remove the twigs and their container and put them in a warm, sunny place. Many of the buds, especially those from maples and willows, will open after a few days. It's a good idea to cut off another 1 cm (0.4 in) from the bottom of the twigs once a week. A clean cut will allow water to enter the stem more easily. On which twigs do the buds open? Is the terminal bud more likely to open than the lateral buds?

Science Fair Project Idea

Measure the average distance between terminal bud scars for different species. Which species grow the most in an average year? Which grow the least?

Chapter 4

Plant Reproduction

FLOWERS ARE OFTEN SO BEAUTIFUL THAT WE FORGET THEIR ROLE IN THE LIFE OF PLANTS. Seeds form in flowers. Many people lose interest in a plant after its flowers fade and wither, but flowers are only one phase—but a very important phase—in the life cycle of a plant. The color and fragrance of flowers attract insects. Insects carry pollen from one flower to another. The pollen contains the plants' sperm cells. Those cells combine with the eggs buried deep within a flower and give rise to seeds and the next generation of plants. Cones play a similar role and also produce pollen to fertilize eggs that develop into seeds. Botanists group plants based on whether they have cones or flowers.

Plants that produce cones are called gymnosperms—commonly referred to as evergreens, conifers, or softwoods. Gymnosperms include pines, spruces, firs, hemlocks, and other trees with needlelike leaves. The word *gymnosperm* means "naked seed." The seeds of gymnosperms are not covered by an ovary (see Figure 17). Gymnosperms produce seeds on scales. The scales are often grouped together as cones. When the seeds of gymnosperms mature and fall, they are not covered but are exposed to the air.

[FIGURE 17]

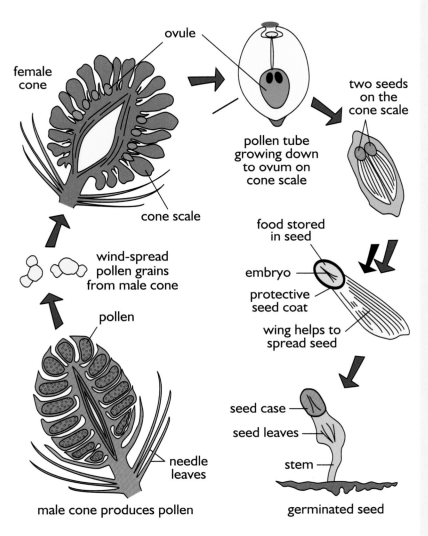

ovule

female
cone

two seeds
on the
cone scale

pollen tube
growing down
to ovum on
cone scale

cone scale

food stored
in seed

wind-spread
pollen grains
from male cone

embryo

protective
seed coat

pollen

wing helps to
spread seed

seed case
seed leaves

stem

needle
leaves

male cone produces pollen

germinated seed

In the life cycle of gymnosperms, sperm and eggs are produced
in separate cones, which may or may not be on the same tree.

Angiosperms, on the other hand, produce flowers. The ovary, which surrounds the seed or seeds, ripens to become the fruit. An apple, for example, is the ripened ovary of an apple blossom. Inside the apple are the seeds. On the outside of the apple you can find traces of its origin from a flower. Look in the dent on the bottom of an apple. There you can see five tiny dry points. These points are the remains of the leaves (sepals) that once held a flower.

Trees that are angiosperms are often referred to as deciduous trees because they lose their leaves for part of the year. (*Deciduous* comes from a Latin word meaning "to fall.") They are also called hardwoods because they produce wood that is harder than the wood of gymnosperms.

There are two types of angiosperms: dicotyledonous plants (dicots) and monocotyledonous plants (monocots). *Dicots* have two cotyledons in their seeds, while monocots produce seeds with a single cotyledon. There are other general differences, too.

In Chapter 2 you learned about the veins of leaves. The leaves of dicots usually have veins that form a network, such as the veins in the leaves of maple trees or bean plants. Monocot leaves usually have veins that are parallel, such as the leaves of corn plants and grasses. The flower parts of dicots usually come in fours or fives or multiples of four or five, whereas monocot flower parts appear as threes or multiples of three.

The wind carries the pollen of most forest trees to other flowers. The flowers of wind-pollinated trees are generally rather drab and have little if any odor. Other trees, such as the cherry, apple, magnolia, willow, and most ornamental trees, produce beautiful flowers with lovely odors. These trees must attract the insects that transport their pollen from flower to flower.

Producing fruit is an advantage to the tree. The fruit enables the seeds to move away from the tree. Berries, acorns, apples, and other fruits are eaten by animals. The seeds pass through the animals' digestive systems and are deposited far from the tree that produced them. Squirrels gather and hoard acorns in the fall. In the process, they lose some in the ground. In effect, they plant the seeds for the oak trees. The likelihood of an acorn being planted and germinating is very small. But seeds are produced in such great numbers that if only one in a million germinates and survives, the oak population will remain unchanged. The same figures are true for most other trees.

Some trees have different ways of spreading their seeds. Alders grow near water. Their seeds contain tiny air-filled bladders. When the seeds fall, many are carried by the water to a damp shore where some of them may germinate. Maples and ash trees produce winged seeds that spin and wobble as they fall, enabling the wind to carry them from beneath the limbs of their parents. The fruit of the witch hazel has a built-in spring mechanism. When the fruit dries and opens, it projects the seeds away from the plant. Willows and poplars have developed what may be the best means of spreading seeds. Their seeds, like those of the dandelion, are light with a fluffy material that acts like a parachute. If caught by the wind, they may be carried for miles.

In the experiments that follow, you will dissect a flower, look closely at pollen grains, and grow pollen tubes. You will examine flowers and cones. You will cut fruits open to reveal the seeds inside. Examining flowers, pollen, cones, seeds, and fruits will help you understand plant reproduction.

4.1 Flower Dissection

The parts of a typical flower are shown in Figure 18a. The *sepals* are the outermost parts of a flower. They are often green and leaflike; however, in some flowers, such as tulips and lilies, the sepals may be the same color as the petals. Sepals protect and cover young flowers before they open. Petals are usually the bright, colorful part of a flower that lie just inside, and often between, the sepals. Sepals and petals are called the accessory parts of a flower because they are not directly involved in producing seeds.

The essential parts of the flower, which are needed to produce seeds, are the stamens and the pistils. The *stamens* consist of long, slender filaments that have little knobs at their ends called *anthers*. Grains of pollen form on the anthers. If you rub your finger across an anther, you may be able to see some fine, yellow dustlike particles of pollen. Perhaps you can collect enough pollen to study under a magnifying glass or microscope.

The *pistil* or pistils, the female part of the flower, are usually at its center. The tip of the pistil, which is called the *stigma*, has a sticky substance that helps collect pollen grains carried to the pistil by insects, wind, water, or gravity. A pollen grain produces a long tube through which sperm cells travel to the egg that is located at the lower end of the pistil shown in Figure 18b. The union of sperm and egg produces an embryo that eventually becomes part of the mature seed.

Flowers that receive pollen from another plant of the same species are said to be cross-pollinated. Generally, cross-pollination produces larger, healthier plants than does self-pollination, in which pollen from a flower's stamens falls on the pistil of the same flower. Two ways that a plant

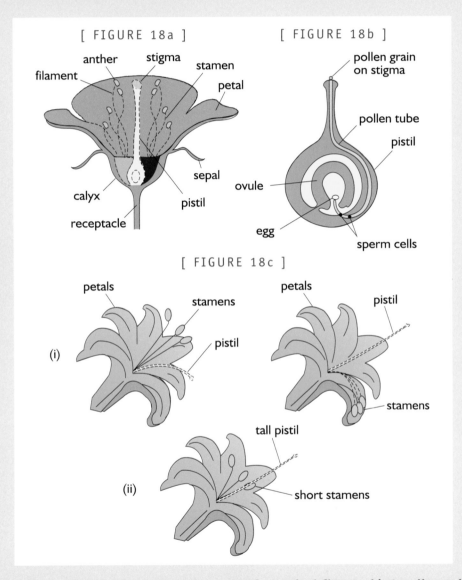

[FIGURE 18a]

anther stigma
filament   stamen
            petal

sepal
calyx   ovule
pistil
receptacle   egg

[FIGURE 18b]

pollen grain
on stigma

pollen tube
pistil

sperm cells

[FIGURE 18c]

petals   stamens
(i)   pistil

petals   pistil
              stamens

tall pistil
(ii)   short stamens

18 a) The drawing shows the main parts of a typical flower. b) A pollen tube
grows down the pistil. Sperm cells move along the pollen tube and fertilize
the egg or eggs in the ovule at the base of the pistil. c) Two ways to avoid
self-pollination include (i) maturation of the stamens and pistils at different times; (ii) tall pistils that reach well above the same flower's stamens.

avoids self-pollination are shown in Figure 18c. Other ways of preventing self-pollination include having flowers with only pistils or stamens, but not both, on any one plant of a species (dioecious plants), chemical incompatibility between pollen and stigmas of the same flower, and a variety of structural mechanisms.

Insects are often attracted to plants with brightly colored petals. Some flowers have glands called *nectaries* that produce nectars, which are sweet liquids with odors that attract insects. Many people also enjoy the fragrance of these nectars. Bees, as you may know, collect nectar, as well as pollen, as a source of food. The pollen that sticks to their bodies is carried from flower to flower with the insects. When the insect bodies rub against the pistil of a flower, some of the pollen sticks to the stigma.

Many flowers are small and drab. They have little color and no nectaries. They may even lack petals and sepals. Such flowers do not attract insects, but they usually produce an abundance of pollen that is carried by wind or water.

Flowers that have all four flower parts—sepals, petals, stamens, and pistils—are called *complete flowers*. Flowers that lack one of the four parts are said to be *incomplete*. Oat flowers, for example, are incomplete because they lack both sepals and petals. Anemone and clematis plants have stamens, pistils, and sepals but no petals. Willows produce flowers that have neither sepals nor petals. Furthermore, their flowers have either stamens or pistils but not both; consequently, willow flowers have only one of the four parts common to flowers.

Flowers with both pistils and stamens, such as tulips, lilies, roses, orchids, and sweet peas, are said to be *perfect*. In some plants, such as willow, oak, and cottonwood trees, the pistils and stamens are found in separate flowers. Flowers lacking either pistils or stamens are said to be *imperfect*. Flowers that bear only stamens are called staminate flowers. Those that bear only pistils are pistillate flowers. Dioecious plants produce imperfect flowers on separate plants. Such plants, some of which bear staminate flowers while others produce pistillate flowers, include willows and cottonwoods. Monoecious plants, such as oak trees and corn, bear both pistillate and staminate flowers on the same plant. The familiar tassels of a corn plant are the staminate flowers, while the silk found lower on the same plant is part of the pistillate flowers.

An oat flower is perfect because it has both stamens and pistils but incomplete because it lacks sepals and petals. Why are all imperfect flowers also incomplete?

The best way to see the parts of a flower is to dissect a large one. A daffodil, lily, snapdragon, or tulip is a good flower to dissect. If you can't find one growing at home, you may be able to obtain wilted ones free at a florist shop if you explain why you need them. Look at the whole flower before you begin dissecting (see Figure 18a). The green, cuplike structure that connects the flower to the stem or receptacle is the *calyx*. The calyx is made up of the sepals. How many sepals are on the flower you are dissecting? Are they green or another color?

The petals make up the colored blossom that most people think of when they hear the word *flower*. How many petals does your flower have? Are the petals and sepals equal in number? Do you think the flower is a monocot or a dicot? Is it perfect or imperfect? Complete or incomplete? How do you know?

Use your fingers or tweezers to carefully remove the petals. You should be able to see the stamens and pistil or pistils found at the flower's center. How many stamens does your flower have? How many pistils does it have? A magnifying glass may help you see the parts more clearly. Draw a picture of the flower you have just dissected. Label the parts of the flower.

4.2 Pollen Grains

Materials:

- flowers or cones that are producing pollen
- black construction paper
- magnifying glass or microscope
- cup
- measuring tablespoon
- sugar
- water
- saucer
- plastic wrap

Find flowers that have pollen on their stamens or collect pine cones that shed a fine yellow powder (pollen) when shaken. Gently shake the pollen onto a small piece of black construction paper. Use a strong magnifying glass or a microscope to look at the pollen grains. Compare the pollen grains from different flowers and cones. How do they differ? Do any resemble those shown in Figure 19a?

Dissolve several tablespoons of sugar in a cup of water. Pour a little of the sugar solution into a shallow saucer. Sprinkle some of the pollen onto the sugar water. Cover the saucer with plastic wrap and leave it in a warm place for several hours.

Examine the pollen grains with a magnifying glass or microscope. Can you see any tubes like the ones shown in Figure 19b growing from the pollen grains? These are the tubes that grow into the pistil and reach the ovules in the ovary.

Korean fir

holly   birch   ash

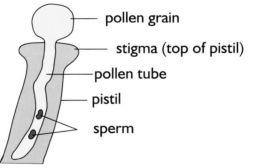

— pollen grain

— stigma (top of pistil)

—pollen tube

— pistil

sperm

19 a) Pollen grains from several different trees are shown. The pollen
has been greatly magnified. The Korean fir pollen grains have
balloonlike air sacs that enable them to almost float in air.
b) A pollen tube grows from a pollen grain and carries sperm to
the egg inside a flower's pistil.

4.3 Seeds of Flowering and Cone-Bearing Plants

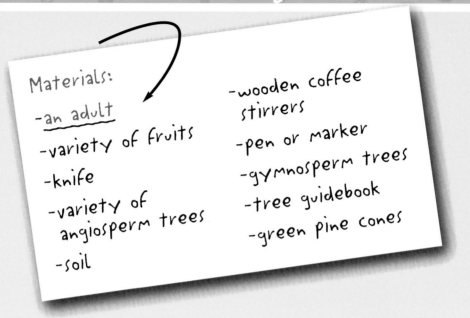

Materials:
- an adult
- variety of fruits
- knife
- variety of angiosperm trees
- soil
- wooden coffee stirrers
- pen or marker
- gymnosperm trees
- tree guidebook
- green pine cones

The seeds of angiosperm trees are found inside the fruit. With time and patience, you can collect a large number of seeds produced by different trees. You know where to look for the seeds of apple, orange, lemon, lime, grapefruit, peach, pear, and cherry trees.

If possible, collect some of the fruits shown in Figure 20. As you can see from the drawings, there are many types of fruit. The words commonly used to describe a fruit do not always agree with the scientific definitions. For example, neither a raspberry nor a strawberry is a true berry. One is an aggregate fruit; the other an accessory fruit. But a tomato is a berry. Can you explain why?

Examine as many different types of fruit as you can. **Ask an adult** to cut open fleshy fruits so you can look inside. Dry fruits can be examined as they are. Can you find the seeds? Can you find any flower parts, other than the ovary, that still remain with the fruit?

Many trees, such as the horse chestnut, oak, beech, black walnut, butternut, pecan, and hickory, produce a fruit called a nut that contains the tree's seed. Can you find any trees that produce nuts?

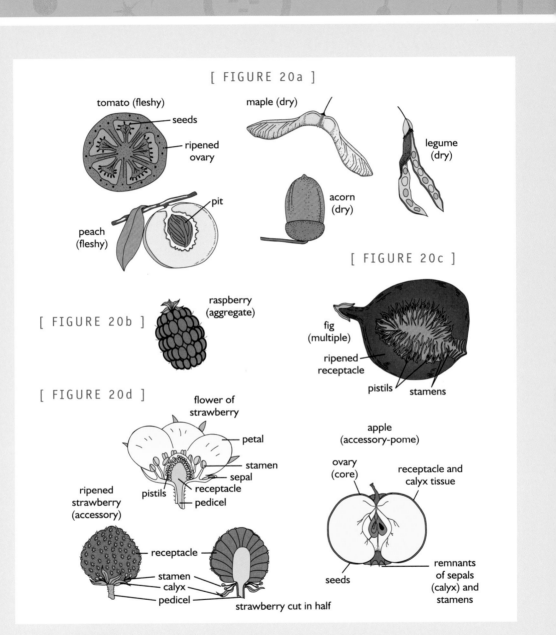

tomato (fleshy)
— seeds
— ripened ovary

peach (fleshy)

maple (dry)

acorn (dry)

legume (dry)

pit

[FIGURE 20c]

raspberry (aggregate)

[FIGURE 20b]

fig (multiple)
ripened receptacle
pistils   stamens

[FIGURE 20d]

flower of strawberry
— petal
— stamen
— sepal
— receptacle
— pedicel

ripened strawberry (accessory)
pistils

apple (accessory-pome)
ovary (core)
receptacle and calyx tissue

receptacle
stamen
calyx
pedicel

strawberry cut in half

seeds

remnants of sepals (calyx) and stamens

20 a) **Simple fruits develop from a single ovary. b) Aggregate fruits are those where several ovaries on the same flower ripen together. c) In multiple fruits many ovaries from separate flowers ripen together on one stem. d) Accessory fruits include parts of the flower or plant other than the ovary.**

If there are maple trees near where you live, look for hanging clusters of their winged seeds late in the spring or in the summer. The seeds eventually fall from the tree. It's fun to watch them spin as they fall. Sometimes the wind carries them far away. How are the seeds from other trees dispersed (scattered) so that they don't grow in the shade of their parent tree?

Locust, catalpa, Kentucky coffee, mesquite, and paloverde trees produce a podlike fruit, similar to pea pods, that have several seeds inside. Look for these pods in late summer. When the pods dry, you can open them and see the seeds inside.

Plant some different kinds of tree seeds in soil. Use a wooden coffee stirrer to label each seed you plant. Do any of the seeds germinate and grow?

The seeds of gymnosperms (evergreens, conifers, softwoods—trees with needlelike leaves) form inside their cones. Once the cones open, the seeds can be found on the scales of the cone or on the ground beneath the tree.

How many different kinds of cones can you find? Use a tree guidebook to help you identify the species that produced them. Are the trees that produced each kind of cone nearby?

Find some pine cones that are still green. Take them into your home or school and let them dry. When the cones are dry and open, you can see the seeds on the scales of the cones.

Chapter 5

Trees

TREES ARE DEFINED AS PLANTS THAT HAVE A SINGLE STURDY, WOODY, PERMANENT STEM AND THAT GROW TALLER THAN MOST OTHER PLANTS. Such a definition is used to distinguish trees from shrubs and bushes, which have many stems and don't grow very tall. You know what trees are, and perhaps you can identify many of the trees that grow in the region where you live.

TREE PARTS

Trees have four distinct parts: (1) the stem, or trunk, with its branches and twigs; (2) the leaves where the trees manufacture food; (3) the roots, which support the rest of the tree and grow down into the soil where they absorb water and minerals; and (4) the flowers of angiosperms and the cones of gymnosperms, which enable trees to reproduce.

The stem or trunk of a tree provides both support and a system of tubes. The tubes transport water and minerals upward and provide a downward path for food.

The outer part of the stem is the bark. The bark is made up of two parts (see Figure 21). The outer bark contains dead cells that protect the living tissues within it. The inner bark contains living cells. Together, these inner cells are known as the *phloem*. The phloem lies next to a thin layer of cells called the *cambium*. The layer of cells that make up the

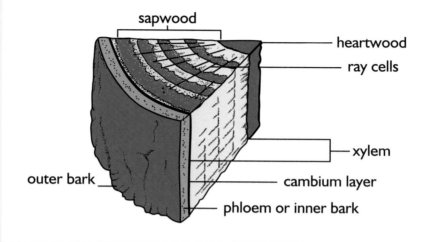

[FIGURE 21]

sapwood

heartwood

ray cells

xylem

outer bark

cambium layer

phloem or inner bark

The drawing shows a section of a tree trunk. Heartwood and sapwood are inside the cambium layer. Phloem cells lie outside the cambium. The outer bark is made up of dead cells that are constantly being shed.

cambium produces phloem cells on its outer side and another type of cell, called *xylem*, on its inner side. The xylem contains a number of different kinds of cells. Some xylem cells transport water and minerals and some food upward from the roots to the leaves. Other xylem cells move water, food, and minerals horizontally across the stem. These are called ray cells. Many xylem cells have thick walls that help to support the growing tree.

Phloem carries mostly food manufactured in the leaves down to the cells of the stem and roots. The role of phloem in conducting food was determined by experiment. When a ring of bark and phloem was removed from a tree trunk, water still reached the leaves above the cut, but food did not reach the cells of the roots or stem below the cut. As a result, the roots eventually died and could no longer absorb water and minerals from the soil. The tree died. The experiment showed that water must move upward to the stem and leaves through the xylem, while food moves downward from the leaves through the phloem.

In older trees, the inner xylem is called the *heartwood*. Heartwood is made up of dead cells that are filled with substances that provide a strong inner core. The cells of the heartwood no longer carry materials up the tree. The outer part of the xylem is the sapwood. It lies between the cambium layer and the heartwood. The xylem cells in the sapwood move water and minerals upward through a tree to the leaves.

In Chapter 1, you learned that roots absorb water and minerals from the soil and transport them to the stem and leaves. But tree roots also have another function. The larger roots hold the tree firmly in the soil. If you have ever seen a tree blowing in a strong wind, you may realize how important a firm anchor in the ground is to a tree.

TREE GROWTH, DISTRIBUTION, AND LIFE CYCLE

Trees grow in diameter. You can see that growth when you look at the annual rings on a tree stump. Each year the cambium layer of cells in the stem produces new phloem cells on its outer side and new xylem cells on its inner side. The xylem cells produced in the spring are large and thin-walled. They make up the lighter part of an annual ring. The xylem cells produced in the summer are smaller with thick walls. Summerwood is the dark part of each annual ring.

At the tips of roots and branches lie tissues that also produce new cells. These cells cause the tree to grow downward, outward, and upward. Trees get longer only at these growing tips. A point on the trunk of a tree where a branch has formed will not move upward. It will remain at the same height above the ground.

Theoretically, trees are immortal, but the oldest known trees are less than 5,000 years old. Most trees do not live more than a century. Forest fires destroy many trees. Others are blown down by high winds or are struck by lightning. Some die during a drought, or humans or beavers cut them down. Trees are also subject to fungal diseases, such as Dutch elm disease, chestnut blight, white-pine blister rust, and many more. Some-times trees are lost to insects that cause them to rot.

Evergreens, such as fir and pine trees, can generally withstand the cold better than deciduous trees, which shed their leaves in the fall. That is why evergreens grow in northern Canada and Alaska (see Figure 22) and

[FIGURE 22]

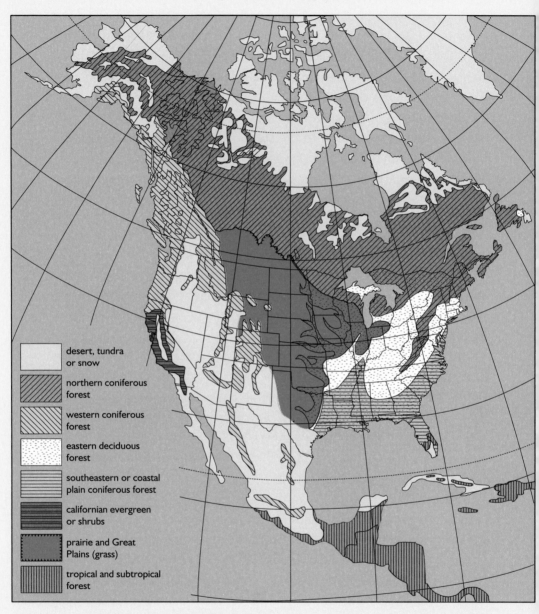

desert, tundra or snow

northern coniferous forest

western coniferous forest

eastern deciduous forest

southeastern or coastal plain coniferous forest

californian evergreen or shrubs

prairie and Great Plains (grass)

tropical and subtropical forest

The major forest areas of North and Central America are shown on this map. Some of the areas overlap. For example, both conifers (evergreens) and deciduous trees (trees that lose their leaves) are found around the Great Lakes.

at high altitudes where temperatures are low. But even evergreens have their limits. They will not grow in regions where temperatures fall to −45°C (−49°F) in the winter.

In addition to favorable temperatures, trees must have moisture and proper soil conditions. Gentle winds help to spread pollen and replenish the carbon dioxide used in photosynthesis, but high winds may remove moisture from trees and reduce growth. Of course, the range of conditions that different trees can tolerate varies. Figure 22 shows the major types of forest areas of North and Central America. In Africa, South and Central America, and southeast Asia, extensive rain forests grow. Some of those rain forests are being destroyed by logging or by burning to make way for more agriculture.

HOW TREES ARE USED

Trees play important roles in our lives. In addition to the shade and beauty they offer, trees hold soil in place and reduce erosion caused by floods or heavy rains. Through photosynthesis, trees provide the food they need to maintain their own growth. In many cases, they also produce the food that makes up the fruits and nuts that are a vital part of our diets. Trees are essential to the paper industry where they are used for the wood pulp from which paper is made. In many parts of the world, wood is the primary fuel for heating and cooking. From trees we obtain the lumber used to build homes and other buildings. Wood has one major drawback as a building material: Can you guess what it is? Despite its flammability, a lot of wood is sawed into lumber because it is light and easy to cut, shape, smooth, and join together. Trees or their wood are also the source of many substances, such as rubber, cellulose, tannins, and resins, which are refined into other products, such as turpentine.

Foresters often measure trees to find out how much lumber can be obtained from the tree. To do that they need to know the tree's height and diameter. A tree's height is also an indicator of its age. If you know the average amount that a particular species of tree grows each year, a tree's height will give you a rough idea of its age. The same is true of a tree's diameter.

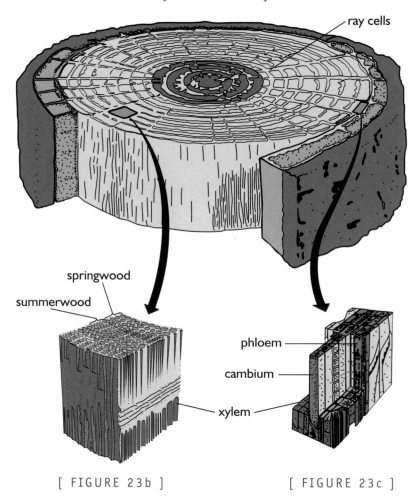

[FIGURE 23a]

ray cells

springwood

summerwood

[FIGURE 23b]

phloem

cambium

xylem

[FIGURE 23c]

23 a) The drawing shows a section of a tree trunk. The dark wood at the center consists of dead cells filled with dark-colored substances. That is the heartwood. The ray cells, which together look like the spokes of a wheel, carry food and water across the trunk. b) This drawing shows an enlarged segment of two annual rings. c) The cambium produces xylem cells on its inside and phloem cells on its outside. It accounts for the sideways growth of the stem.

The cells of the older wood near the center of a tree are dead. They form the tree's heartwood. If air can reach the heartwood, it decays and the tree becomes hollow. Hollow trees can live for many years, but they lack the heartwood's strength.

The sapwood surrounding the heartwood is made up of xylem cells that carry water and minerals up the tree. Most sap flows in the new (most recently formed) ring of xylem cells. If those cells become blocked by a fungus, as they do in Dutch elm disease, the tree may die. The older sapwood cannot carry enough fluid to keep the tree alive. Figure 23 shows a tree's heartwood and sapwood.

Materials:

- rope
- meterstick (yardstick)
- tall trees
- sun
- a friend
- pencil

There are several ways to measure a tree. One way is to measure its height. Another way is to measure the thickness (diameter) of its trunk. Still another way is to measure its girth or circumference, which is the distance around the tree's trunk. Some trees grow very tall. Some redwood trees grow to heights of more than 100 m (330 ft). The circumferences of sequoia (Sierran redwood) trees may reach nearly 30 m (98 ft), which means their trunks are 9 m (30 ft) in diameter.

Look for the biggest tree around your school or neighborhood. Measure the tree's circumference with a piece of rope and a meterstick, or yardstick (see Figure 24). Place the rope around the base of the tree's trunk. Pick up the ends of the rope and wiggle it back and forth until it is at eye level. Grip the rope at the point where one end meets the rest of the rope. Place the rope on the ground. Use the meterstick (yardstick) to measure the length of the rope that went around the tree. What was the circumference of the tree you measured?

Since most tree trunks are basically round (circular), it is not necessary to measure the diameter of a tree's trunk. You can calculate it from the tree's circumference. For any circle, the diameter is equal to the circumference divided by a constant number called π (pi). The value of π is approximately 3.14, but 3 is close enough for estimating the diameter of a tree, which is seldom a perfect circle. What is the approximate diameter of the tree you just measured?

There are several ways to find the height of a tree. If the sun is shining, you can use the length of the tree's shadow and the length of the shadow of an upright meterstick or yardstick to find the tree's height. The sun's light rays are nearly parallel when they reach the earth. As a

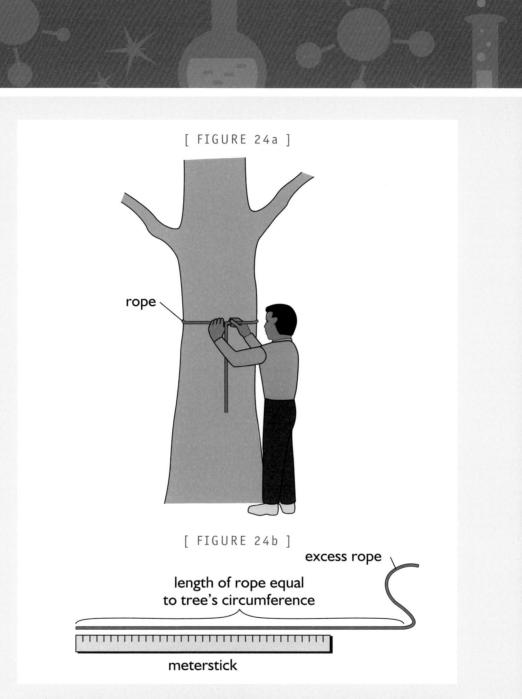

rope

[FIGURE 24b]

excess rope

length of rope equal
to tree's circumference

meterstick

24 a) To measure a tree's circumference, wrap a rope around the tree
at eye level. Mark the point where one end of the rope meets the
rest of the rope. b) Use a meterstick to measure the length of rope
that matches the tree's circumference.

result, the tree's height divided by the length of its shadow has the same value as the stick's height (100 cm) divided by the length of its shadow (see Figure 25a). Why must both shadows be measured at approximately the same time?

Suppose the length of the meterstick's shadow is 50 cm. Then the height of the stick is twice the length of its shadow. The height of the tree, therefore, must also be twice the length of its shadow. If the tree's shadow is 10 m long, its height is 20 m. What will be the length of this tree's shadow when the meterstick casts a shadow that is 25 cm long?

If the sun is not shining, you can use a method used by artists to measure a tree's height. Have a friend stand next to the tree you want to measure, while you stand about 20 m (65 ft) away. Hold a pencil upright at arm's length, as shown in Figure 25b. Line up the top of the pencil with the top of your friend's head. Holding the pencil steady, move your thumb along the pencil until it is in line with the bottom of your friend's feet. The distance between your thumb and the top of the pencil represents your friend's height as seen from about 20 m away. Next, determine how many of these lengths are in the tree's height. You can do this by moving the pencil upward one length at a time.

By knowing how tall your friend is, you can find the approximate height of the tree. For example, suppose your friend is 1.5 m (4 ft, 11 in) tall and the tree, according to your measurement with the pencil, is ten times as tall as your friend. The height of the tree must be

$$10 \times 1.5 \text{ m} = 15 \text{ m, or } 49 \text{ ft}$$

Measure the height and circumference of a number of trees in the area where you live. Try to measure the heights of a number of different kinds (species) of trees, such as maples, pines, oaks, poplars, or whatever species you can find. Choose trees with approximately the same diameter. Does one kind of tree seem to grow taller than others? Do any tend to be shorter than others?

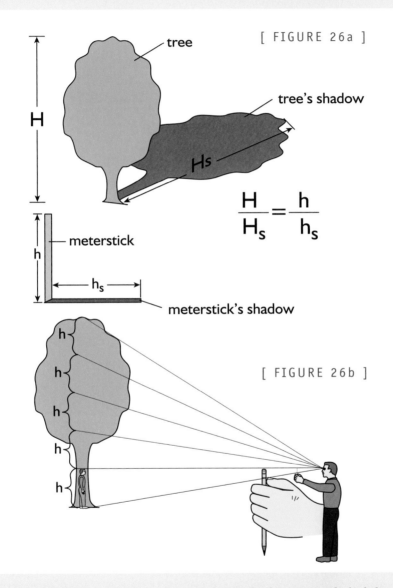

tree

tree's shadow

H

Hs

$$\frac{H}{H_s} = \frac{h}{h_s}$$

meterstick

h

h_s

meterstick's shadow

[FIGURE 26b]

h

h

h

h

h

25 a) The shadow method can be used to calculate a tree's height.
b) The artist's method of estimating the height of a tree is shown.
In the drawing, the tree is five times as tall as the person standing
next to it.

5.2 How Old Was That Tree?

Materials:
- tree stump
- sheet of white paper
- crayon or soft pencil
- firewood
- tree branches

To find the approximate age of a tree, count the annual rings, like those shown in Figure 26. The tree adds a new ring every year. Each ring has two parts, as was shown in Figure 23b. The wider, lighter part (springwood) is made up of cells that are added in the spring when the tree grows rapidly. The thinner, darker part of the ring (summerwood) is formed during the rest of the year when the tree grows more slowly.

Unfortunately, you can't see the rings until the tree is cut down. Foresters and research scientists use fine augers (hollow drills) to cut

[FIGURE 26]

This photograph shows a tree that has been cut. You can see the annual rings inside the tree.

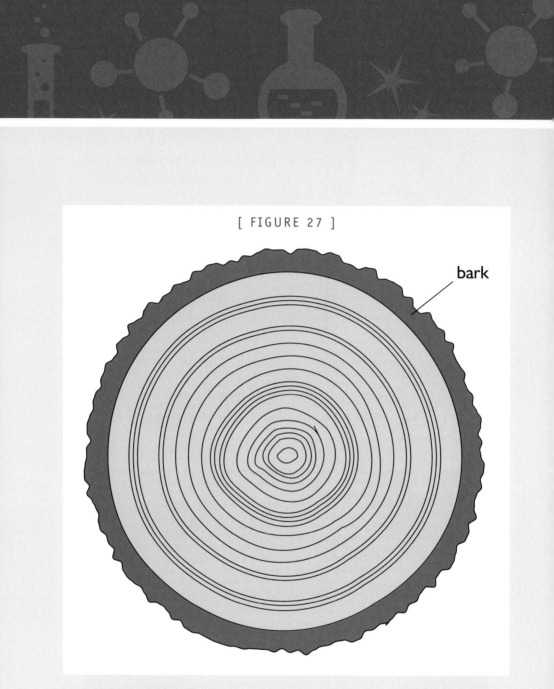

[FIGURE 27]

bark

How old was this tree when it was cut down? During which years did it grow a lot? During which years did it grow very little? Try to explain why it grew more in some years than in others.

out small cores from a tree. The cores can then be used to count the annual rings. But even the annual rings may not give a tree's exact age. If a hurricane, tornado, or other event tears the leaves off a tree, the tree will sometimes grow and lose a second set of leaves in the same year. Such a tree will form two growth rings in the same year.

Although you don't have the fine auger used to take core samples from a tree, you can still see annual rings. Find a tree stump. You will be able to see the annual rings and count them. How old was the tree when it was cut down? How can you tell the years during which the tree grew a lot? How can you tell the years during which the tree grew very little? How can trees reveal past weather patterns?

Use a sheet of white paper and a crayon or soft pencil to make a stump rubbing. Place the sheet of paper on the stump and hold it steady. Be sure the paper is large enough to cover the top of the stump. Rub the side of the crayon or the side of the pencil point back and forth over the paper across the entire stump. Can you see the annual rings in the rubbing?

Look at the drawing of the top of a stump in Figure 27. How old was the tree when it was cut down? In which years did the tree grow rapidly? In which years did the tree grow slowly? What might have caused its slow growth?

You can also see annual rings on firewood. Look for tree rings at the ends of unsplit logs in a woodpile. Can you tell the age of the tree from which the log came?

Perhaps you can find some branches in a pile of firewood, or maybe you can find branches that have broken off a tree during a storm. Do branches have annual rings? If they do, can you predict how the number of annual rings in higher branches compares with the number in lower branches?

5.3 How Many Leaves Are on a Tree?

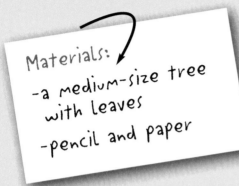

Materials:
- a medium-size tree with leaves
- pencil and paper

One answer to the question "How many leaves are on a tree?" might be "Lots of them!" But you can do better than that. You can make a reasonable estimate of the number of leaves on a tree.

To begin, count and record the number of leaves on several typical branches of a tree. To find the average number of leaves on a typical branch, add the number of leaves on all the branches you counted. Then divide this total by the number of branches examined. What is the average number of leaves on a branch?

Next, count the total number of branches on the tree. How can you use the average number of leaves per branch and the total number of branches to estimate the number of leaves on the tree? What is your estimate of the total number of leaves on the tree?

Make an estimate of the total number of leaves on all the trees on your street.

5.4 How Much Surface Area Does a Leaf Have?

Materials:
- leaves from a tree
- sheet of graph paper, preferably with 1-cm squares
- pencil

The total surface area of a tree's leaves is important because photosynthesis occurs in the leaves. The greater the surface area, the greater the amount of food that can be manufactured in the leaves.

To find the surface area of a typical leaf, collect a number of leaves from one of the trees whose leaves you counted in the previous experiment. Place one of the leaves on a sheet of graph paper. Use a pencil to draw the outline of the leaf on the graph paper.

What is the area of one of the squares on the graph paper? For example, if the squares are 1.0 cm on a side, each square has an area of 1.0 square centimeter (1.0 cm × 1.0 cm = 1.0 sq cm). If the squares are 0.5 cm on a side, the area of each square is 0.25 sq cm (0.5 cm × 0.5 cm = 0.25 sq cm).

Count the number of squares covered by the typical leaf. (In some cases, you will have to estimate the fraction of one or more squares that are partially covered by the leaf. Add those fractions to the squares that are totally covered by the leaf.) What is the approximate area of one leaf in square centimeters? How can you estimate the total surface area of all the leaves on a tree?

Materials:
-trees of the same species located in different places

Watch a number of trees of the same species over a period of one year or longer. Choose trees that are both large and small. Choose trees that are located in different places, such as a hill, a valley, a shady place, a sunny place, a wet place, a dry place, on the edge of a forest, inside a forest, or on a lawn. In your science notebook, make a map showing the location of your trees. Number each tree on the map. Notice and record such things as the time that leaves and flowers first appear on each tree; the time that leaves first begin to turn color in the autumn; the amount that the tree's branches grow in one year; the side of the tree that is growing fastest and the side that is growing slowest; the trees that have the largest leaves; and other differences that you notice as you watch your trees.

Can you explain why one tree develops leaves first? Does it receive more light than the other trees? Does it receive more moisture? Is it more protected from the wind than the other trees?

🏆 Science Fair Project Idea

Try to find possible explanations for the observations you made. Then design experiments to test your explanations. Do any of your experiments confirm your explanations? Do any of your experiments indicate that your first explanation was wrong? Do your experiments lead to other explanations?

FURTHER READING

Books

Bochinski, Julianne Blair. *The Complete Workbook for Science Fair Projects.* Hoboken, N.J.: John Wiley and Sons, Inc., 2004.

Friedhoffer, Bob. *Everything You Need for Winning Science Fair Projects.* Broomhall, Penn.: Chelsea House Publishers, 2006.

Moorman, Thomas. *How to Make Your Science Project Scientific.* Revised Edition. New York: John Wiley & Sons, Inc., 2002.

More, David and John White. *The Illustrated Encyclopedia of Trees.* Second Edition. Portland, Oreg.: Timber Press, Inc., 2005.

———. *World Book's Science and Nature Guides: Trees of the United States and Canada.* Chicago: World Book, Inc., 2007.

Internet Addresses

Andrew Rader Studios. *Rader's Biology4Kids.com.* 2008.
http://www.biology4kids.com/files/plants_main.html

How Stuff Works, Inc. *Plant Activities for Kids.* 2008.
http://home.howstuffworks.com/plant-activities-for-kids.htm

United States Department of Agriculture Research Services. *Science 4 Kids.* 2008.
http://www.ars.usda.gov/is/kids/plants/plantsintro.htm

INDEX

A

angiosperms, 72, 80–82
anthers, 74

B

bark, 83–84
botany, 5
bromthymol blue, 37–38
buds, 51, 66–68

C

calyx, 77
carbon dioxide production, 37–39
centrifugal force, 23–24
chlorophyll
    development, light effects on,
        30, 40
    extraction of, 36
    overview, 5, 29, 34
chromatography, 29, 41–42
cones, 5, 11, 70, 82
cotyledons, growth and, 18–21

D

dicots, 31, 72
dormancy, 11

E

evergreens, 85–87
experiments, designing, 6–7

F

flowers
    classification of, 76–77
    dicots vs. monocots, 72
    parts of, 74–77
    in reproduction, 5, 11, 70
fruits, 72–73, 80–82

G

germination
    factors affecting, 16–17, 40
    overview, 11–15
    soil type and, 22
gravity effects, 52–54
growth
    cotyledons and, 18–21
    factors affecting, 22–24, 52–54
    measurement of, 68
    of roots, 23–24, 61–65
    in stems, 23–24, 52–54, 59–60
    of trees, 85
gymnosperms, 70, 82

H

heartwood, 85, 89

I

insects, 70, 76

L

leaves
    development, 51
    light effects, 30, 40
    overview, 5, 29
    quantifying, 98–99
    scars, 68
    starch, testing for, 34–36

stomata, 29, 43, 49
transpiration, 43–49
veins in, 31–33, 72
light effects, 30, 40

M

monocots, 31, 72

N

nectar, 76
nutrients, 18–21, 56–58

P

palmate venation, 31
parallel venation, 31
petals, 74
petioles, 31, 58
phloem, 84
photosynthesis
carbon dioxide production by,
37–39
leaf surface area, 99
overview, 5, 29, 34
pi (π), 90
pigments, testing for, 29, 41–42
pinnate venation, 31
pistils, 74
plants, 5, 25–26
pollen, 70, 74–76, 78–79
pollination, 70, 72, 74–76

R

reproduction
cones in, 5, 11, 70, 82

flowers (*See* flowers)
overview, 5, 11, 70–73
seeds, dissemination of, 72–73
in trees, 11, 70–72
respiration, 34, 37
roots
development, 18, 51
growth of, 23–24, 61–65
trees, 83, 85

S

safety, 9
sapwood, 85, 89
science fairs, 8
scientific method, 6–7
seeds
dissemination of, 72–73
germination (*See* germination)
overview, 11
plants, growing from, 25–26
scarring of, 13
sepals, 74
springwood, 95
stamens, 74
starch, testing for, 34–36
stems
growth of, 23–24, 52–54, 59–60
nutrient transportation in,
56–58
origins of, 18, 51
stomata, 29, 43, 49
summerwood, 85, 95